D1603480

Performing

Whiteness

THE SUNY SERIES IN
POSTMODERN CULTURE

Joseph Natoli, *Editor*

PERFORMING WHITENESS

Postmodern Re/Constructions
in the Cinema

WITHDRAWN

GWENDOLYN AUDREY FOSTER

State University of New York Press

Published by

STATE UNIVERSITY OF NEW YORK PRESS, ALBANY

© 2003 State University of New York

Printed in the United States of America

For information, address
State University of New York Press,
90 State Street, Suite 700, Albany, NY 12207

Production by Marilyn P. Semerad
Marketing by Patrick Durocher

Library of Congress Cataloging-in-Publication Data

Foster, Gwendolyn Audrey.
   Performing whiteness : postmodern re/constructions in the cinema / Gwendolyn Audrey Foster.
      p. cm. — (SUNY series in postmodern culture)
   Includes bibliographical references and index.
   ISBN 0-7914-5627-7 (alk. paper) — ISBN 0-7914-5628-5 (pbk. : alk. paper)
      1. Whites in motion pictures. 2. Race relations in motion pictures. 3. Social problems in motion pictures. I. Title. II. Series.

PN1995.9.W45 F67 2003
791.43'655—dc21

                                                                          2002029182

10 9 8 7 6 5 4 3 2 1

For Wheeler

CONTENTS

ILLUSTRATIONS

Acknowledgments

My heartfelt thanks to the organizers of the Center for Culture and History of Black Diaspora at De Paul University, who invited me to speak at the Colloquia Series "Framing the Black Diaspora: Crossings, Belongings, Presence"—held in the Spring of 1998—where I first presented "Albert Schweitzer: The Great White of Lambaréné: A Study of Whiteness through a Decolonized Gaze." Many thanks to the organizers of the conference "Moving Images: Technologies, Transitions, Historiographies," held at the University of Stockholm in 2000, where I first presented a paper on queer performativity in Claire Denis's *Beau Travail*. Thanks also to the organizers of the conference hosted by *Literature/Film Quarterly*, the International Literature/Film Association Millennium Conference, held in the summer of 1999 at the University of Bath, where I first presented my paper on Alice Guy Blaché's *Making an American Citizen*. I also wish to thank the audience members, whose comments were invaluable in rethinking my work on this difficult film. The Pioneer Women's Film Project at Duke University, organized by Jane Gaines, has also been a great influence in my work. I thank the project for all their great work in promoting the study and preservation of work by early women filmmakers and for organizing a special panel held at the Society for Cinema Studies Conference in Palm Beach in 1999, where I delivered a paper on Alice Guy Blaché's film *La Vie du Christ*. Again, the audience members who made comments during that presentation led me to rethink the film in terms of its depiction of race. My deepest gratitude goes to the UNL Research Council, who awarded me with a grant to travel in the summer of 1999 to film archives in New Zealand and Amsterdam to view rare film prints. I wish to thank the members of the Department of English at the University of Nebraska, Lincoln, for their support of my work, and the many writers and theorists who have influenced my thinking on the subject of whiteness. I wish also to thank the members of the class I offered in postcolonial approaches to film theory in 2001. Your fascinating discussions and honesty taught me a great deal about the complexity of whiteness. All the material in this volume is original, with the brief exception of my discussions of The "Great White" of Lambaréné, which appeared in slightly different form in Popular Culture Review 11.2 (Summer 2000): 113–19; my thanks to Felicia Campbell, editor; and my discussion of Alice Guy Blaché's film La Vie du Christ, which also appeared in considerably different form Film Criticism 23.1 (Fall 1998): 6–17; Lloyd Michaels, editor. For her help in preparing and typing this text, I wish to thank Dana Miller for her assistance during this long and arduous task, as well as Kathryn Koldehoff, whose contribution to the completion of this text is deeply appreciated. I thank Wheeler Winston Dixon, my husband, for his patience, support, and helpful comments on early drafts of this manuscript.

CHAPTER ONE

PERFORMING WHITENESS

The history of moving pictures is a living record of performances of whiteness, class, gender, and myriad identity markers, such as sexuality, nationality, and ethnicity. It is ironic and fascinating that, in the face of the biological evidence that race really doesn't exist, more than a century of filmic performances of whiteness would appear to insist on the existence and visual supremacy of whiteness. With the end of the twentieth century, the rise of "whiteness studies" worked to destabilize the assumptions behind whiteness as a cultural norm. The work of many critics, especially Richard Dyer, called into question the "norm" of whiteness, noting that those who do not fall into the white category are marked as *other* while, "at the level of racial representation, in other words, whites are not of a certain race, they're just the human race" (*White* 3). More recently, Kalpana Seshadri-Crooks argues that whiteness should not describe a group or race; it should instead be seen as a *term* that makes the logic of race thinking possible. Seshadri-Crooks wishes to shake up notions about race in her psychoanalytic study of whiteness, *Desiring Whiteness: A Lacanian Analysis of Race.*

> We must develop a new adversarial aesthetics that will throw racial signification into disarray. Given that race discourse was produced in a thorough visual culture, it is necessary that the visual itself be used against the scopic regime of race. . . . I am proposing an adversarial aesthetics that will destabilize racial looking so that racial identity will always be uncertain and unstable. (158–59)

In keeping with Dyer, who sees his project as "making whiteness strange" (*White* 4), I also wish to make whiteness strange by studying the performance of whiteness in moving pictures and other forms. My project is a postmodern attempt to reconstruct, deconstruct, and examine the performance of whiteness in moving images. The performance of whiteness in cinema may be viewed as a sort of cultural, repetitive-stress dis-ease, a place where we can return to the repressed, the disordered, and the destabilized; whether that be whiteness, class, or compulsory heterosexuality, the cinema is a factory of identity performances. It is the garment center of white fabrication. The cinema has been remarkably successful at imposing whiteness as a cultural norm, even as it exposes the inherent instability of such arguably artificial binaries as male/female, white/black, heterosexual/homosexual, classed/not classed. It is as though the cinema has sought to hold up these binaries with an almost unrelenting fervor that insists on the definition of the body through performance.

Whiteness does not exist at the biological level. It is a cultural construct, yet whiteness defines us and limits us. I don't believe in whiteness, yet I am writing a book about the performance of whiteness in moving images. I don't believe in whiteness, yet I am supposed to be white. I am defined as such, and, to perform American whiteness correctly, I am expected to erase all signs of my hybrid ethnicity: Irish, Dutch, African American, and Native American. The tenets of postmodernism apply to the study of whiteness. Jean Baudrillard's concept of the simulacrum as a copy lacking an original *(Simulacra)* can be applied to whiteness. The failed search of white supremacists and others for a "lost pure white race" proves this point. Whiteness lacks an original, yet it is performed and reperformed in myriad ways, so much so that it seems "natural" to most. It is taken for granted—the norm that is unmarked. To question whiteness is to question the air around us; it's always there, but nobody acknowledges it. But air is real, unlike whiteness, which has no biological basis. Jean-François Lyotard defines postmodernism as a questioning of all master narratives (see Jameson xii).

Whiteness is a master narrative that is increasingly being questioned and marked. Postmodernists reconfigure identity as a performance that is itself fractured, unstable, and mutable. White performances are simulacra, falsely stabilized by master narratives that themselves are suspect, and whiteness itself is a construct that needs constant upkeep. It is in the cracks and fissures of performative whiteness that we can begin the dismantling of whiteness as norm. A postmodern approach exposes cracks and fissures in whiteness and white performativity. The scope of this study is wide and uses postmodern pastiche. Thus I discuss films across all genres, from sci-fi classics to more recent blockbusters. I introduce a concept of "whiteface" and connect it to what I call *white space*, a postmodern concept of on-screen space where identity is negotiated, mutable, and transitory. I discuss such notions as white minstrelsy, whiteness as its own other, and on-screen performances of the good-white body and the bad-white body. I connect white performativity to consumer identity. I discuss class issues and the practice of "class-passing," as well as related issues, such as race, sexuality, and ethnicity. In this book I employ performance studies, cultural studies, and other newly emerging disciplines. These disciplines displace the supremacy and artificial hegemony of auteur studies, psychoanalytic studies, and even to some extent spectatorship studies. While these approaches are often quite useful, theorists sometimes forget to take into account the wider cultural significance of the performing white body that supports the supremacy of the norm of whiteness. Just like race and racism, films are a *coproduction* of time, place, culture, authorship, desire, spectator mediation, and acting, among many other factors and forces, including such institutions as the Motion Picture Production Code, but drawing from a wide range of sometimes unstable hegemonies. Performance gives the *illusion* of stability, but we should always remember that performance is a fabrication, a fake that has become a necessity in the regime of identity markers in the cinema. Judith Butler speaks to the issue of performance as an organizing principle of identity.

> According to the understanding of identification as an enacted fantasy or incorporation, however, it is clear that coherence is desired, wished for, idealized, and that this idealization is an effect of a corporeal signification. In other words, acts, gestures, and desire produce the effect of an internal core or substance, but produce this *on the surface* of the body, through the play of signifying absences that suggest, but never reveal, the organizing principle of identity as a cause. (173)

Even before the birth of cinema, it is clear that the visual representations of whiteness were already difficult to maintain. Early photographic manuals reveal the instability of whiteness and the lengths to which practitioners went to establish white as the norm, and the goal of lighting was "the elimination of shadow" (*White* 96). Richard Dyer—in addition to presenting an astute discussion of cinema lighting, emulsion, and aesthetics, all of which are designed to stabilize and capture whiteness on film and/or videotape—details the extent to which photographers and cinematographers went to fabricate whiteness in performers. Under the harsh, hot arc lights, film actors in classic Hollywood films were forced to wear thickly applied white makeup, causing them to sweat profusely under this performative facial mask. This unpleasant makeup was also used in everyday performance of whiteness, especially in the early twentieth century. It is worth noting that whites went to great lengths to foster the public's acceptance of the construct of whiteness, which is clearly an artificial and *performed* "norm." For the purpose of public performance, either live or on the screen, it seemed that white people themselves were not quite *white* enough. To create the illusion of whiteness, they needed to be covered with gluelike white face paint and perform in a sort of whiteface. The concept of whiteface, then, while significant, has largely been unexplored in recent critical theory, while blackface performativity justifiably has been the subject of intense cultural scrutiny. Whiteface not only includes, in my estimation, unnaturally white makeup but also careful lighting and an insistence on the binaries of black and white, especially notable in the early films of Lillian Gish and Mary Pickford, to use Dyer's examples. Actors in early cinema were not just pressed into service to construct genres, genders, sexualities, and classes; they faked and seemingly "normed" a look of whiteness that is itself a grotesque parody, a parody as bizarre, in a way, as that of blackface. This practice persists to the present day in television, theatrical, and motion picture makeup, which artificially whitens the color of a white artist's skin, to make the performer seem "whiter than white," an irresistible presence on the screen or stage. I agree with Valerie Babb, who writes, "[O]nly by coming to a full awareness of the ways in which an artificially crafted identity was constructed to maintain hierarchy and divisiveness can any meaningful and useful dialogue on race begin" (5–6). Coming to awareness includes the recognition of whiteness as a performed construct. One proof of the constructedness of whiteness is the comedy of Chris Rock, Eddie Murphy, and Margaret Cho, who all do impressions of white performance. Such comics point out the artificiality of speaking, walking, and generally performing whiteness.

Some might claim that it will be impossible to disturb the category of whiteness. Indeed, there is plenty of evidence of whiteness's continuing to avoid the radar screen of cultural and social consciousness when it comes to discussions of race. Invoke the word *race* and you invoke, for most listeners, images of the "nonwhite other." In my daily life as a "white" professor, I teach predominately "white" students. Confronted with topics about race, most of my students opt out of the discussion, as if they have no race, no ethnicity, and no investment in the stakes of race as social discourse and the construction of race in the cinema. Confronted with the idea of white privilege, "white" students sometimes respond with jealousy: "I don't really have a culture," one student told me. Students also claim disinterestedness, or they display guilt, which Dyer and others have pointed out is a "blocking emotion" (*White* 11). While teaching a course in postcolonialism, I had great success in destabilizing "white" students' notions of whiteness in conjunction with examining colonial jungle films, such as *King Kong* (1933), *She* (1965), and *Tarzan, the Ape Man* (1932). As the course progressed, students became increasingly comfortable with othering whiteness and studying the ways in which whiteness has been introduced, rehearsed, and performed in colonialist cinema. Whiteness might be *presumed* to be a stable category that eludes study, but whiteness can indeed be made strange in the same way that heterosexuality can be displaced as the norm, made strange. Perhaps I am overly optimistic, but I must agree with Babb, who predicts the inevitable fall of the category of "whiteness": "Ultimately, the insularity that whiteness needs to maintain itself—the self-absorbed conversations, the moving only within a set of like people, the exclusive living enclaves—will become difficult to maintain" (172).

The realization that race is largely a cultural construct and that both *homosexuality* and *heterosexuality* are terms and norms that are relatively new and easily destabilized suggests a new paradigm for undermining the notion and category of whiteness. As C. Loring Brace persuasively argues, "[T]he concept of race does not appear until the trans-Atlantic voyages of the Renaissance" (qtd. in Saulny 3). "There was no whiteness prior to the seventeenth century," agrees Manning Marable. "Whiteness is the negation of something else. The something else are Africans who are described by Europeans not by their religion or nationality but by the color of their skin. And nowhere in Africa did Africans call themselves 'black'" (qtd. in Saulny 3). Dr. Ife Williams details how, as the colonial process moved forward in the 1600s, "people with dark skin were demonized in order to justify their exploitation. The people in power spread the belief that '[t]hese people are nothing but monkeys. We're helping them out'" (qtd. in Saulny 3). Similarly, the categories and binaries of heterosexuality and homosexuality were not named or concretized until the late nineteenth century, when the "proclamation of the homosexual's existence preceded the public unveiling of the heterosexual" (Katz 54). In fact, it seems to have taken at least a few decades for there to be an agreement on the meaning of the terms, and initially *heterosexual* was a term associated with perversion or "non-procreative perversion" (54). The emphasis was on procreation, and procreation was seen as the norm. Any other motive for sex was once seen as perverse; even the first uses of the term *heterosexual* were associated with perversion.

> The earliest-known use of the word *heterosexual* in the United States occurs in an article by Dr. James G. Kiernan, published in a Chicago medical journal in May 1892.
>
> *Heterosexual* was not equated here with normal sex, but with perversion—a definitional tradition that lasted in middle-class culture into the 1920s. Kiernan linked heterosexual to one of several "abnormal manifestations of the sexual appetite"—in a list of "sexual perversions proper"—in an article on "Sexual Perversion." (Katz 19)

Thus heterosexuals were once seen as "deviants"; their worst inclinations were toward "modes of ensuring pleasure without reproducing the species" (20). This emphasis on reproduction of the species is matched only by the doggedness seen in early cinema that worked to maintain and perform whiteness. Indeed, the stabilization of the white heteronormative goes hand-in-hand and is deeply connected, according to Dyer.

> Race and gender are ineluctably intertwined, through the primacy of heterosexuality in reproducing the former and defining the latter. It is a productively unstable alliance. . . . *Whites must reproduce themselves,* yet they must also control and transcend their bodies. Only by (impossibly) doing both can they be white. Thus are produced some of the great narrative dilemmas of whiteness, notably romance, adultery, rape and pornography. (*White* 30; my emphasis)

White heterosexuals are thus expected to reproduce themselves. Homosexuality remains suspect to many because homosexual acts do not result in procreation.

Just as it took a great deal of time and effort to define and maintain whiteness, it took quite a bit of effort and time to invent and maintain the norms and binaries of heterosexuality and homosexuality, only to see these categories disrupted and destabilized by bisexuality, transvestism, intersexuality, and the transgendered, not to mention the persistent campaign of queer (and straight) activists who continue to campaign against a culture of compulsory heterosexuality. We may still live in a world of white dominance and heterocentrism, but I think we can agree that we are in the midst of postmodern destabilizing forces when it comes to sexuality and race. Though the dominant cinema and the media continue to norm whiteness and heterosexuality, it seems to take Herculean effort to maintain the binaries necessary to stabilize white heterotopia and supremacy. Many scholars, thinkers, and activists are actively challenging the visual systems that result in othering. Just as black activists remain committed to displacing white visual utopias that seek to other them, whites need to begin to challenge the validity of whiteness, question white privilege and norming, and study the images and performances that seek to define them.

In *The Color of Sex* Mason Stokes notes that "whiteness and heterosexuality can be usefully seen as analogous structures—normative copartners in the coercions of racial and sexual power" (191). A quick glance at contemporary mainstream cinema reveals, perhaps not surprisingly, an emphatically white heterocentric world. *The Mummy Returns* (2001) revolves around a heterosexual white couple (Brendan Fraser as action-figure hero Rick O'Connell and Rachel Weisz as the equally athletic Evelyn Carnahan O'Connell) and their adventures into the world of the "other," a predictably Orientalized mixture of Egyptian, Arab, and unidentifiable ethnic types. They are aided by a grinning, snaggletoothed, black British aviator, who whisks them out of danger with his hot-air balloon. This character, Izzy, played by Shaun Parkes, performs no function in the film other than fulfilling the needs of the central white couple and their equally white blond son, Alex (Freddie Boath). If this scenario reminds you of countless films that rely on a similar formula, it should: this is a formula that makes white American viewers feel comfortable. It places black maleness safely to the side. The nonthreatening, nonsexual, black other performs not only as buddy, servant, and helpmate but also as a necessary ingredient in the film's racial makeup to fully mark the whiteness of the nuclear family in the film and, by extension, the white audience.

Rick O'Connell, in addition to having his black buddy, also enjoys the services of his effeminate brother-in-law, Jonathan Carnahan (played by John Hannah). Obviously coded as gay, this character serves as a safely neutral other to the central couple's performative heterosexuality. Jonathan is the butt of most of the jokes of the film; he is an ineffectual bumbler in the style of the movie "pansies" of the 1930s, a stereotype that John Hannah plays to the hilt. The Jonathan character is also greedy, and on several occasions he places various members of the cast in peril, due either to his avarice or to his negligence. Near the end of the film, for example, Jonathan, by reaching for a final piece of precious archaeological treasure, almost tips over the hot-air balloon in which Rick, Evelyn, and Alex are escaping. Izzy and Jonathan also must spend time arguing over the loot that they have illegally acquired, in true colonialist fashion, thus demonstrating the goodness and civility of Rick, Evelyn, and Alex, who are not out for colonial loot but rather for pure science. Nevertheless, Jonathan can be counted upon when truly needed: in one pivotal scene Jonathan helps Alex restore life to Evelyn by using the boy's knowledge of Egyptian hieroglyphs.

The Mummy Returns thus readily, even eagerly, conforms to the white hero-black buddy-queer sidekick formula that reaches back into the moribund imagination of Hollywood and the machine of whiteness, which is exemplified in hundreds, perhaps thousands, of mainstream films. In *King Kong* (1933) the great white hunter (Carl Denham [played by Robert Armstrong]) and his heterosexual love interest (Ann Darrow [Fay Wray]) seek to capture a great black ape on Skull Island, an obviously fabricated jungle. Fay Wray's white female goddess Ann is made to appear whiter than white through lighting, blondness, and clothing, but it is the threat of black male sexuality and miscegenation that blatantly reifies her whiteness. King Kong himself is a stand-in for the threat of black male sexuality: as Thomas Doherty notes, when King Kong is brought to America, he is "chained and sedated below the decks of the expeditionary ship" (290), an enslaved black body not unlike a slave on his way to serve white America. The white actors perform the central quest of the narrative. Their performances are marked by routine assumptions of white privilege and mistreatment of those who are forced to serve them.

Scores of other white American films have featured the "good black" buddy-servant in such disparate productions as *Trader Horn* (1931), which features not only an "African" manservant, played by Mutia

Omoolu, but also a Latino protégé, Peru, played by a decidedly effeminate Duncan Renaldo. In both cases the nonwhite other is included in the
narrative to emphasize the bravery, intelligence, and effective heteroper-
formativity of the white male adventurer and the beauty and sexual
supremacy of the virginal white female. In *Casablanca* (1942), one of the
more famous films of the 1940s, we find African American Dooley Wilson as Sam, the faithful piano player in Rick's Café, along with effeminate
Vichy functionary Claude Rains as Captain Louis Renault, *aiding* the
white heterosexuals Rick Blaine (Humphrey Bogart) and Ilsa Lund Las-
zlo (Ingrid Bergman) in their battle against the Nazis. *Casablanca* is thus
a white film about white people in war-torn Morocco under the Vichy
regime. If it were a film about African Americans during the Civil War,
such as *Glory* (1989), it would be carefully marked (and marketed) as a
"black film." Even in such a black film, of course, we learn about the
bravery and heroic efforts of a white Northerner, Colonel Robert Shaw
(played by Matthew Broderick), who plays a more significant role than
the supporting actors who play the first unit of African American soldiers
to fight in the Civil War. Denzel Washington (as Private Trip), Morgan
Freeman (as Sergeant Major John Rawlins), and the other African American actors perform blackness as defined by the militaristic code of heroism, but it is always done in the service of white American supremacy.
Indeed, Matthew Broderick was praised for his performance, almost as if
his performing whiteness in the confines of a black film was special and
heroic in itself. In the *Lethal Weapon* films Danny Glover plays Roger
Murtaugh, the black sidekick for Mel Gibson's heroic white cop, Martin
Riggs. The black female sidekick also frequently aids whites with their
white problems in such films as *Boys on the Side* (1995) and *Ghost* (1990),
the celebrated white heterocentric vehicle in which Sam Wheat (Patrick
Swayze) "borrows" Whoopi Goldberg's blackness (in the character of the
semifraudulent medium Oda Mae Brown) to communicate with his
fiancée, Molly Jensen (Demi Moore). Even white ghosts from the dead
can count on the service of blackness. The task of listing all of the films
in the white American canon that emphatically trade on blackness to
help, fix, and mediate white heterosexual fantasies would be monumental
and impossible. One might expect more recent films to limit the reliance
on the black helper, but this is not the case.

In *Pearl Harbor* (2001) white American cultural icons Ben Affleck,
Josh Hartnett, and Kate Beckinsale are aided by Cuba Gooding, Jr., an

actor who by all rights should be commanding the salaries of the top-paid actors and ought to be able single-handedly to open a blockbuster, but his blackness works against him in white-controlled Hollywood and white America. So far, Gooding is acceptable to white America in secondary roles but not in central, leading roles. Don Cheadle is another African American actor who ought to be the lead character but is often relegated to the role of the sidekick, best friend, or enabler of white folks. Cheadle's accomplished performance in *The Rat Pack* (1998) as Sammy Davis, Jr., demonstrably proved that he is capable of delivering a stellar performance, but Hollywood and its audiences have yet to allow him the opportunity to open a big-budget vehicle, such as *Pearl Harbor*. But if Cheadle had been the lead in *Pearl Harbor*, the film would probably have been considered a black film and then would probably have been relegated to low-budget status. Hollywood executives are not always correct in their assumptions about audiences. *Pearl Harbor* did not do the business that was expected. But the surprise hit of the summer of 2001 was *Rush Hour 2*, a film that does not feature a white leading man, couple, or buddy team. *Rush Hour 2* features Hong Kong action star Jackie Chan and top-billed African American comedian Chris Tucker in a culture-clash comedy that tapped into a "hidden" but enthusiastic audience. Meanwhile, most of the summer fare offered in 2001 suffers from a sort of race profiling that is routinely practiced in Hollywood casting and performances. The feature-length cartoon film *Shrek* (2001) uses Eddie Murphy's voice to give life to an animated donkey, who serves as a sidekick to an ogrelike animated character voiced by Mike Myers, in pursuit of the heart of Princess Fiona (Cameron Diaz). Martin Lawrence gets top billing over Danny DeVito in the comedy *What's the Worst That Can Happen?* (2001), but only because Lawrence is also one of the executive producers of the film. White Americans have always been comfortable with African Americans as comics, who are routinely used as cultural and social stereotypes in the service of Hollywood's hegemonic white cinematic discourse. Orlando Jones (as Dr. Harry Block) is thus prominently featured in photos, television spots, and theatrical trailers for *Evolution* (2001) stereotypically popping his eyes and grinning to advertise the film. Yet Jones is billed after a white actor, David Duchovny, known for his television work with aliens and "others" on *The X Files*. Disney's *Atlantis: The Lost Empire* (2001) is a vehicle for white performativity to engage with the otherness of supposed lost civilizations, and Steven Spielberg's *A.I. Artificial Intelli-*

gence (2001) allows white actors Haley Joel Osment (as the adorable child cyborg David) and Jude Law (as Gigolo Joe) likewise to engage in otherness, here enacted within the genre formulas of science fiction, a zone in which issues of race can be evaded or subverted, which perhaps explains audience acceptance of Tim Burton's remake of *Planet of the Apes* (2001). Given white culture's history of equating Africans and African Americans with apes, *Planet of the Apes* offers yet another "comforting" example of whites donning black ape-face with cultural impunity. The original *Apes* series, begun in 1968 with *Planet of the Apes* and ending in 1973 with *Battle for the Planet of the Apes,* not counting the many spin-offs in television movies, animated cartoons, and even a short-lived series, proves that the concept is both durable and perennially popular.

In the many *Tarzan* films whites found an opportunity to critique white colonialism but also to engage in resuscitating the missing link in the Darwinian chain: the white male (most famously played by Johnny Weissmuller) who was raised in the jungle. When Weissmuller's Tarzan was retired, he became Jungle Jim in the long-running series of cheap *Jungle Jim* films of the early 1950s. Tarzan's and Jungle Jim's heroism are seen as equal to that of other "good natives," such as Mowgli (played by Sabu) in *The Jungle Book* (1942) and Bomba (Johnny Sheffield) in the popular *Bomba* films made in the late 1940s and 1950s for juvenile (and mostly male) white American audiences. White viewers, through Sheffield, Sabu, Weissmuller, and the heavily camouflaged actors in the many *Planet of the Apes* films, are allowed, paradoxically, to perform otherness, as well as other whiteness. In short, they are encouraged temporarily to leave whiteness behind and to engage in a hybridity that is otherwise discouraged and was even unallowable under the original Code. Not only was race mixing, also known as "miscegenation," forbidden by the Motion Picture Production Code, but specific rules were set out that clearly marked the zones of the white body that were allowed to be shown. By setting films in "exotic" locales, and by playing out fears and fantasies of race mixing in the genre of the adventure—or jungle—film, whites invented a zone in which the Code's rules no longer enslaved them. Though they were still subject to the Code, film producers pushed the envelope as far as possible in the *Tarzan* films and in subsequent jungle films. As in the *Tarzan* series, the *Planet of the Apes* films allow white audiences a form of fantasy, an escape from the white "civilized" body of colonialism and consumption, and an idyllic return to nature. Both types of films have enjoyed

12

FIGURE 1. Johnny Weissmuller as the white king of the jungle in *Tarzan, the Ape Man* (1932). Courtesy Jerry Ohlinger Archives.

considerable box-office success, perhaps because, as Walt Morton suggests, "a large part of the . . . audience enjoys a narcissistic identification with the power-fantasy suggested by Tarzan's strength and command of nature" (113). Perhaps the *Apes* films are much like the *Tarzan* films to white audiences, for, as Dyer comments, "With *Tarzan,* the white man can be king of the jungle without loss of oneness to it. *Tarzan* films effect an imaginary reconciliation between the enjoyment of colonial power and the ecological price of colonialism" (*White* 158).

White scientists have long been fascinated with the relationship between apes and humans, and this fascination is clearly equaled by a racist fascination with the supposed close connection between Africans and apes. This trope reoccurs in the *Planet of the Apes* films, but added to this white cultural mythmaking is an attempt to get a grip on American historical struggles having to do with race. Rather than deal head-on with these struggles, whites prefer to deal with such issues in the sci-fi or adventure genre vehicles that Hollywood regularly churns out with renewed vigor and hype. As Ed Guerrero wrote in 1993 of the *Planet of the Apes* quintet, "The struggles and reversals between futuristic apes and humans form a sustained allegory not only for slavery but also [for] the burdens of racial exploitation, the civil rights movement, and the black rebellion that followed it" (43). Perhaps more importantly, these films bring up the specter of slavery without making the white viewer at all uncomfortable. Whites are even able to distance themselves smugly from their colonial past and have the spectatorial pleasure of being removed from the history of slavery and racial and economic colonial exploitation. As Guerrero asserts, "[S]lavery's sedimentation can be [as] momentary and [as] fleeting as a sentence or a musical refrain threaded into the film's soundtrack" (43).

Without an interest in sustaining fantasies about evolutionary development and unspoken fears of racial difference, the maintenance of the *Planet of the Apes* films would be impossible, but few white critics seem aware of the underpinnings and assumptions of these films. Londa Schiebinger writes extensively about the fascination with apes in the seventeenth century and during the Middle Ages, noting that, "Humans— part brute, part angel—were thought to link the mortal world to the divine" (80), and there was much discussion of whether apes could think, speak, reason, or even have table manners. Carolus Linnaeus actually ranked one type of ape "in the same genus as humans . . . [though] most naturalists maintained that while apes might bear human characteristics, they certainly were not human" (81). Linnaeus also noted that apes were clearly good at parenting. Other naturalists noted that apes mourned their dead. But apes' inability to speak placed them below humans on the evolutionary scale, even though some early naturalists insisted that apes were capable of speech. Perhaps more important than the question of speech was the question of whether apes were able to be civil and were civilizable. The horrifying truth is that the same questions were applied to Africans themselves, and most readers should be familiar with the exhibition of Africans such as Sarah Baartman (otherwise known as the "Hottentot Venus"), who was displayed in Europe in the nineteenth century to "prove" the anatomical difference between Europeans and Africans. White spectators could poke and prod her anatomy and note her supposed large buttocks and genitalia. Baartman was not the only human to be put on display in such a ghastly manner. Humans of non-European extraction were viewed as indigenous ethnographic specimens, to be displayed and examined as one would display and examine any other scientific specimen. As Fatimah Tobing Rony comments, "At the beginning of the [twentieth] century, a Chirichiri man named Ota Benga from the Kasai region of what is now Zaire was exhibited at the Bronx Zoo" (158). Benga, along with other "human specimens," was also on display at the St. Louis World's Fair and the American Museum of Natural History in New York, where he lived. It is notable that Benga was displayed in the "monkey house" (Rony 158) at the Bronx Zoo. In addition, ethnographic "specimens," especially Native Americans and Africans, were put on visual display in countless ethnographic films, including the ethnographic fiction film, still celebrated today in film circles, *Nanook of the North* (1922). It seems as if white moviegoers in the earliest years of the twenty-first century are as fascinated with a ranking of races and the desire to find a missing link between man and ape as they were in the seventeenth, eighteenth, nineteenth, and twentieth centuries.

Tim Burton's *Planet of the Apes* draws on these fascinations and returns the apes to their proper place as noble savages. As Bill Desowitz notes in a *New York Times* preview of the film, Burton is "an old hand at bizarre reversals and the blurring of primitive and civilized behavior" (30). According to Desowitz, "indigenous humans can talk in this version, though instead of caged beasts they are now slaves and pets" (30). Most interesting is that white actors, such as Helena Bonham Carter, play the parts of the beasts. Bonham Carter plays a chimpanzee human rights activist, while Tim Roth plays a tyrannical chimpanzee. The point of the film is that humans can be overtaken by another intelligent species, but the film can't be disentangled from its racial politics. Nevertheless, Desowitz emphasizes the special effects of the film.

> But the apes in the new film hardly resemble their predecessors. Technological advances in makeup design have allowed Rick Baker to go way beyond John Chambers's ground-breaking, Oscar-winning work in the original film. Mr. Baker's creatures look and act more like real apes. They are faster, quicker and more powerful. (Desowitz 3)

Like the *Tarzan* films, *Planet of the Apes* offers a place for whites to perform the other in an imaginary exotic locale, once again effecting an imaginary reconciliation between the races and a safe place to consider the wages of slavery and colonialism, but the film is at once both a reminder of race relations and a token pacifier for the white audience.

The *Planet of the Apes* series operates at the fringes of the scientific discourse of primate studies, for, as Donna Haraway argues,

> The primate field, naturalistic and textual, has been a site for elaborating and contesting the bio-politics of difference and identity for members of industrial and post-industrial cultures. Cloning is simultaneously a literal natural and a cultural technology, a science fiction staple, and a mythic figure for the repetition of the same, for a stable identity and a safe route through time seemingly outside human reach. Evolutionary biology's bottom line on difference is succinctly stated . . . [thusly:] in the end, non-identity is antagonistic; it always threatens the survival of cooperative relationships. In the end, only the sign of the Same, of the replication of the one identical to itself, seems to promise peace. (368–69)

This primal story is of the constructedness of whiteness and the fear of its instability; or, as Michael Atkinson puts it, regarding the original *Planet of the Apes,* "[S]omewhere under the skin the central ordeal of [Charlton] Heston's missing link is one we face only in our darkest dreams" (9). The films themselves exist in the boundaries of racist primate constructs, forcing "you to discount any respite from the relentless dialectic of oppression because it all leads you to a genocidal *auto-da-fé* we've already witnessed" (14). To some extent, the *Planet of the Apes* cycle asks

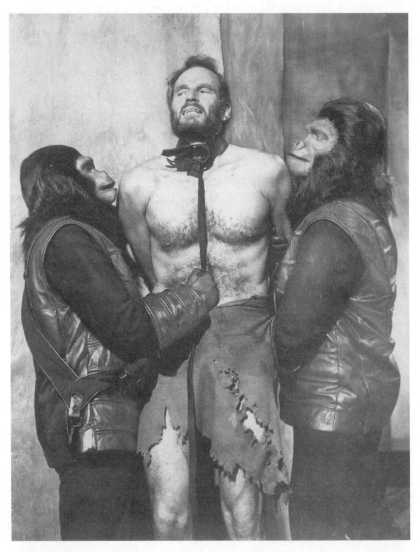

FIGURE 2. Charlton Heston as a slave in the original version of *Planet of the Apes* (1968). Courtesy Jerry Ohlinger Archives.

the white viewer to make whiteness strange and to engage in self-othering. The director of the original film, Franklin Schaffner, points to the mirroring and self-othering effect that he intended: "Hopefully, it worked on the level that you were sitting and watching a simian society functioning, and it occurred to you, suddenly that you were in a hall of mirrors, looking at yourself" (qtd. in Sobchack, *Screening* 182). This self-reflexivity fluctuates with fear, and it is interesting that humans are the dominated species in most of the *Planet of the Apes* films. Clearly, then, as Eric Greene proposes, "[T]here is a long-standing fear among whites in the United States of an 'exchange of situation; a loss of racial domination'" (25). Thus we have Tim Burton's stab at the same old white narrative that amounts to collective white America's novel form of self-reflective navel gazing, mirroring, and simultaneous distancing from culpability.

If the *Planet of the Apes* saga ultimately results in stabilizing whiteness, does cybertechnology, genetic science, and the very unscientific practice of counting people by racial category work to foster a sense of stability or instability when it comes to whiteness? Ironically, the census system, which has been overhauled and reworked to include more ethnic types and now allows people to check more than one racial or ethnic type, exposes the limits of race thinking in the United States. People may now call themselves both black and Native American or both white and Native American, for example. But according to Steven A. Holmes of the *New York Times,* "[T]he overwhelming bulk of the 6.8 million people who listed themselves as multiracial—will be counted as members of the minority" (1). Holmes notes that such logic is an extension of the three-fifths compromise, wherein framers of the U.S. Constitution "reached a compromise to count black slaves as three-fifths of a person" (1), and is also reminiscent of the one-drop rule. Counting one's race is a subjective matter, as is being counted by race. The Los Angeles Police Department, in response to the public outcry against racial profiling and racial harassment, is now required collectively to "record what they perceive is the race, ethnicity, or national origin of each driver they stop" (Rodriguez 1), but most notably they must record this "data" "without asking a direct question" (1). How are officers supposed to guess a person's race or national origin? The powers that be have apparently agreed that straightforwardly asking citizens their race is out of the question. "[A]ll agree that explicitly asking people their racial background would only worsen the tensions between the police and the communities they serve" (5). Besides, as Margo J. Schlanger, a professor at Harvard Law School, states, "We're not trying to get at truth, we're trying to get at bias" (qtd. in Rodriguez 5). Confusion, slippage, and a rather subjective postmodern sense of what constitutes racial or ethnic identity are the markings of a nation of destabilized notions when it comes to race and identity. Even though this scorekeeping, this counting, is obviously not scientific, nor is it in any way objective, it is often treated as such, whether it is for politically motivated statistics, medical research, data for redistricting, or crime statistics according to race. Gregory Rodriguez notes that

> the abolition of racial data is as likely to eradicate the national obsession with race as widespread racial monitoring will make Americans less race-conscious. A frontal assault on race statistics could also provoke the opposite reaction, reinforcing the very demographic categories that racial privacy advocates believe already hold too much sway over American life. (5)

If whiteness remains the norm, if whiteness itself is not broken down into ethnic categories, as in the census and in racial profiling, whiteness remains falsely stabilized, while other racial and ethnic identities are destabilized. Perhaps it is true then that, as Andy Goffey writes, "difference is something that no amount of representation, no amount of mediation by subjective consciousness, will ever manage to pacify, and the inconvenience with which any ethics has to deal is precisely that" (65). Perhaps Americans wish to sidestep the issue by embodying cyberfantasies as nonracially marked cyberspecies in such video game-styled feature films as *Tomb Raider* (2001), and *Final Fantasy: The Spirits Within* (2001). Nevertheless, the synthespians appear to be white, thus explaining the casting of Angelina Jolie as Lara Croft in the film version of *Tomb Raider*. For all of the talk of the computer age as a time in which we can fool around with subjectivity, pretend to be other races and genders, or embody Deleuze and Guattari's notion of the "body without organs" (149), it seems as if our cyberworlds are populated mostly by white peoples' mirror images.

The world of cyberidentity isn't all that different from the real world, as is clear in the recent rise of egg-donation "services" on the Internet. In "Eggs for Sale," a profile of the new business of human egg marketing, author Rebecca Mead follows the life of a Columbia Law School student who sells her eggs. The woman is described as a "nice girl: she doesn't drink, she doesn't smoke, she doesn't take drugs, she's pretty and quick to

laugh, and she has a lovely singing voice" (56). Without even being told, we *know* she is a white woman because it is not our custom to mark white women as such, only nonwhite women get marked in our white-centric culture. But just in case we missed that nonmarking, we learn of this woman's success at donorship. "On both occasions, she had been selected as a donor immediately, no doubt because she is fair and blue-eyed and has a good academic record" (56). In this description whiteness and class are denarrated. In other words, they are not narrated, but they are assumed. She who is fair and blue-eyed is obviously white, though it is unstated. The reference to the academic record implies both class significance and the assumption of privilege and intelligence. If the donor were an African American, she would be clearly marked and labeled as either black or African American.

Feminists have long struggled with the tendency to conflate *woman* with identity as *white woman*. Such exclusionary practices have been scrutinized most clearly by black feminists and by postcolonial scholars who note that, as a group, the term *women* often connotes only a group of white women. This phenomenon is omnipresent in American culture. A recent article in *Esquire* on the patenting of genetic materials is pointedly accompanied by a two-page spread of a blond, white, nude woman, and, on the cover of the magazine, another airbrush-perfect white woman coyly poses holding one arm across her breast, while her other arm carefully covers her vagina. The article explores the manner in which the U.S. Patent Code covers genetic material, but it is clearly presented as a narrative of alarm and titillation for the presumably male readership of *Esquire*. The blurb before the article is meant to disturb the viewer as he is confronted with the display of the nude white female body.

> The U.S. patent code was never meant to cover your genes, your cells, your blood, or the marrow in your bones. But it does. And Craig Venter's map of the human genome was never meant to lead to the kind of great gene rush that is taking place as you read this. But it has. And the worst thing is, it's too late for you to do anything about it. You've already been sold. (Hylton 103)

This material appears in a box, much like the surgeon general's warning appears in a cigarette ad. The object of pleasure (white woman/cigarette) is ruptured by the display of the warning (your genes have been sold/cigarettes kill). The essay itself, by Wil S. Hylton, is a brilliant exposé of the history of genetic patenting. Human genes are being patented, as are gene sequences and mice for cancer research. The colonization of bodies, a remnant of the culture of slavery, is going on with the aid of the Supreme Court, which in a number of decisions has ruled in favor of various genetic companies. It is clear that we do not own our own genetic material, that we are all, in a sense, owned by science. What surprises Hylton most, however, is the public's relative silence on the matter, even as it acquiesces to a new order of biological determinism that is ruled by economics and, to a large extent, existing racial prejudice (160).

Underscoring the artificiality of "whiteness" as a construct is the work of the Human Genome Project, which seeks to map the vast human genetic fabric. Not surprisingly, the project is a controversial one, even within the small group of scientists who are conducting the research. As Nicholas Wade outlines the ethical problem facing the National Human Genome Research Institute, the central question facing the researchers is whether one ethnicity is more predisposed to certain types of diseases than others.

> With the decoding of the human genome largely complete, government scientists are beginning to construct a special kind of genetic map that would provide a shortcut to locating variant human genes that predispose people to common diseases.
>
> The question the scientists face is whether that map should chart possible differences that may emerge among the principal population groups, those of Africans, Asians and Europeans. (17)

The director of the institute, Dr. Francis Collins, hopes to create a genome map "in a fashion that benefits human kind and doesn't unwittingly do damage to one population or another" (qtd. in Wade 17). And yet, as another researcher associated with the project, Dr. Eric S. Lander, commented, while "we must make sure the information is not used to stigmatize populations[,] . . . we have an affirmative responsibility to ensure that what is learned will be useful for all populations. If we shy away and don't record the data for certain populations, we can't be certain to serve those populations medically" (qtd. in Wade 17).

Though these scientists are concerned about the potential marginalizing effects of their research upon certain factions of the world's populace, they also hold out the possibility of a fascinating trump card—that the research will reveal more about human commonality than racial difference. As Lander asserted, "I think these data have tremendous potential to deconstruct simplistic notions of race and ethnicity" (qtd. in Wade 17), a comment echoed by Dr. Phyllis Epps, another researcher associated with the Human Genome Project. "If we educate the public properly it will undermine the traditional concepts of race, and race will begin to fall by the wayside in the traditional sense," Epps argued (qtd. in Wade 17), based on the scientists' discovery that "the genomic map now being envisioned . . . is based on an emerging discovery that the cards in the human genome have been far less finely shuffled than was expected" (Wade 17). Or, as Lander put it more succinctly, "[I]n the end we may conclude none of these identifiers add much" (qtd. in Wade 17). The increasing likelihood of the commonality of the human building blocks is yet another indication that the artificial constructs of race imposed by society for centuries may at last be crumbling.

Meanwhile, we are subject to Spielbergian contemplations of the promise of mastery and innovation in genetic science with the release of the film *A.I.* In Spielberg's world intelligence is defined and performed through the vehicle of an artificial white "boy." A huge ad in the *New York Times* describes his whiteness by denarrating it:

> David is 11 years old.
> He weighs 60 pounds.
> He is 4 feet, 6 inches tall.
> He has brown hair.
> His love is real.
> But he is not. (*A.I.* 7)

Again, intelligence is defined as white, and whiteness is associated with cyborg subjectivity. The cyborg white other is symptomatic of America's fear of the death of whiteness, coupled with whites' attempt to co-opt genetic reproduction as a means of keeping whiteness alive, even in science fiction and in alternative cyborg realities. Dyer's fascination with whiteness as death in sci-fi films, especially the *Alien* trilogy, speaks to the issue of the reproduction of whiteness: "The suspicion of the emptiness of whiteness and also of its terminal reproductive line is crucial . . . [and] may suggest [that] the suspicion of nothingness and the death of whiteness is, as far as white identity goes, the cultural dominant of our times, that we really do feel we're played out" (*White*

217). David in *A.I.* is a *phantom.* He's not real, even if he's white, eleven years old, sixty pounds, four and one-half feet tall, brown-haired, and intelligent. We can no longer believe our senses or our emotions; artifice is omnipresent.

In *Osmosis Jones* (2001), the latest (white) body-function comedy from Bobby and Peter Farrelly, Chris Rock plays the title character, Osmosis Jones, a courageous *white* blood cell who seeks to protect his human host, Frank Pepperidge (Bill Murray), from the effects of a common cold, with the aid of Drixorial, or "Drix" for short (David Hyde Pierce). In *Osmosis Jones* the white body (known by its inhabitants as "The City of Frank") is seen as a vehicle for comedy through instability, as Frank's uncontrollable, dis-eased, white body almost kills Osmosis Jones and Drix before stability is predictably restored in the film's closing moments.

The instability of race and the fantasy of colonization of the body is at the core of so many of our fantasy films that we are obviously collectively revisiting notions of evolution, colonialism, the body, and identity itself. As its predecessors did, *Jurassic Park III* (2001) maroons a group of (mostly) white people on an island populated with ancient DNA-fabricated prehistoric animals, with predictably disastrous results. *Final Fantasy: The Spirits Within* centers on the quest of Dr. Aki Ross, the cinema's first entirely artificial synthespian, to find the essential spirits of human life and thus restore a balance between the citizens of earth and the alien others who steal their energy. *The Animal* (2001) stars Rob Schneider as Marvin, an "everywhiteman" in a transspecies transplant comedy that expands the sociocultural arena of race mixing into an interspecies taboo. *The Animal* traffics in bestiality humor, as Schneider flirts with farm animals and mimics animal behavior while still maintaining his cinematic constructedness as a white, privileged male. In the comedy *Evolution* a meteor hits the earth, bringing with it rapidly mutating forms of alien life that soon threaten the survival of humankind. But perhaps there is no better example of the cinema's current preoccupation with interspecies gene blending than the character the Scorpion King, portrayed by whitened, digitized real-life WWF wrestler Dwayne Johnson, "The Rock," crossed with a mammoth scorpion, who confronts the white British anthropologist and her husband in *The Mummy Returns.* In all these films performing whiteness is problematized by fears and fantasies of interracial dis-harmony, interspecies disaster, and a return to Victorian colonialist narratives of the great white adventurer, colonialist expansionism, medical adventurism, and genetic colonialism.

Yet for all its seeming instability, white performativity and white normativity still reign supreme. The mass-audience success of the Eurocentric throwback *Gladiator* (2000) was equaled for teen audiences by the Heath Ledger vehicle *A Knight's Tale* (2001), in which Ledger plays the role of a valiant young knight, William Thatcher. *A Knight's Tale* might more properly be dubbed "A White's Tale," as the film's nearly all-white cast return us to the white Eurocentric trope of mythic and heroic medieval splendor, a fairy tale of a white heterotopia that is billed as "a blend of *Gladiator* and *Shakespeare in Love*" (1998), as described by critic Andrew Johnston of *US Weekly* in the full-page ad for the film in the *New York Times* (*Knight's Tale* 2). The reference to these two white films signifies that this is, after all, a comfortable white man's (or boy's) tale. An article about Ledger in *GQ* (which caters to a white male readership) stresses Ledger's average "white guyness." Though much is made of Ledger's Australian identity, he is portrayed as a hard partier, a white male as American as apple pie, fit to do battle with his cinematic opponent, Count Adhemar (Rufus Sewell), who isn't black but wears black to signify his status as evil. As described in *GQ,* Ledger, at twenty-two,

> is regarded as the Total Package: soulful and skillful; adept with muskets, swords and horses; highly plausible in period garb; and possessed of a smile that may well open movies. Taken together, his gifts translate into potentially enormous revenues for the studios that employ him—which is what makes Heath Ledger Hollywood's white knight du jour. "His best attributes as a person are his best attributes as an actor," says Rufus Sewell, the movie's dastardly, black-armored baddie. "The fact that he's a really good, kind, brave, clever fellow is what comes across in his work. He warms up the screen." (Erdmann 171)

Whiteness is once again associated with goodness, kindness, and intelligence. Ledger is pointedly dubbed here "Hollywood's white knight du jour." The film itself is nothing more than a rehash of *Prince Valiant* (1954), in which a young Robert Wagner indulges in almost exactly the same series of tropes as Ledger's character does in *A Knight's Tale* but without the rock-and-roll soundtrack. Being a knight, apparently, is mediated by being white, even in 2001.

24

FIGURE 3. Heath Ledger as the good-white knight in *A Knight's Tale* (2001). Courtesy Jerry Ohlinger Archives.

CHAPTER TWO

INVENTING WHITENESS

Whiteness as a construct was already in place at the end of the nineteenth century when photography and cinema began their respective histories. Certainly, whiteness has been a category in flux since very early times. Most interesting in examining whiteness in the cinema, though, is the peculiar rise of a falsely stable American whiteness, which was created at the expense of hybridity. Grace Elizabeth Hale writes of the collective cost Americans have paid as a result of displacing hybridity.

> That both whites and blacks, or more broadly all people of all colors, cannot truly embrace the range of North American humanity as their own, as their imagined community, is the collective cost. Making whiteness American culture, the nation has forgone other possibilities. The hybridity that could have been our greatest strength has been made into a means of playing across the color line, with its rotting distance of voyeurism and partisanship, a confirmation of social and psychological division. (10)

The history of the invention of whiteness in America has been well documented and continues to be a source of investigation. The very definitions of liberty, freedom, and citizenship in American society are highly dependent on seventeenth- and eighteenth-century white-skin privilege laws, laws that falsely separated laboring-class people by color. Early America was a sloppy amalgamation in terms of color and class privilege, with a mixture of bond laborers of different ethnic backgrounds, black slaves, white owners, and even free blacks. As Theodore W. Allen explains in *The Invention of the White Race,* stability needed to be created so that free whites could be carefully separated from black slaves to provide for the safety and the hegemony of capitalist agriculture. "The solution was to establish a new birthright not only for Anglos but for every Euro-American, the 'white' identity that 'set them at a distance' . . . from the laboring-class African Americans, and enlisted them as active, or at least passive, supporters of lifetime bondage of African Americans" (248). Thus, liberty and citizenship in America, from its inception, depended on being white and free. Allen notes that, as early as the seventeenth century, there was "a marked tendency to promote a pride of race among the members of every class of white people[;] to be white gave the distinction of color even to the agricultural European American bond-servants, whose condition in some respects was not much removed from that of actual slavery" (249). That meant that the formerly "black Irish" and other "mongrel races" of European descent were separated culturally and legally from African American slaves and bond laborers. As Michael Rogin asserts, the history of the construction of whiteness relates directly to the idea of American freedom in cinema, for, "when American film takes its great leaps forward, it returns to its buried origins. Then it exposes the cinematic foundations of American freedom in American slavery" (16). Clearly then, whiteness is a form of social control that erupts and continues to be reinvented in cinema. The white race, supported by laws based on skin color, was invented primarily as a form of social control, and it would be up to all forms of popular culture, including vaudeville, theater, and motion pictures, to maintain and further the construction of whiteness. It is thus important to remember that, as Allen asserts, social control is at the center of whiteness.

> Thus was the "white race" invented as the social control formation whose distinguishing characteristic was not the participation of the slaveholding class, nor even of other elements of the propertied classes. . . . What distinguished this system of social control, what made it "the white race," was the participation of the laboring classes: non-slaveholders, self-employed small-holders, tenants, and laborers. In time this "white race" social control system begun in Virginia and Maryland would serve as the model of social order to each succeeding plantation region of settlement. (251)

Lest we begin to think that elements of social control of the white-race system are in the past, we need only look to the current news for examples of the rigid enforcement of conformity displaced as allegiance and telling examples of race-based discrimination that directly address the issue of freedom as still being a white-skin privilege. On 6 June 2001, CNN News presented a special segment of its series *TalkBack Live* in which audience members and e-mail subscribers are given the opportunity to speak out about the issue presented. Bobbie Battista, the host, explained at the top of the program that state representative Henri Brooks of Tennessee, an African American woman legislator, refused to stand and say the Pledge of Allegiance in the chamber with the other representatives because, for her, the flag represents a country that once sanctioned slavery and continues to allow racial discrimination. Apparently the head clerk of the chamber asked her either to stand or to leave because there were children in the chamber who might (supposedly) get the wrong idea. It was interesting to read the e-mail responses of the audience. Although some people noted that the flag is supposed to represent the freedom *not* to stand and say a pledge of allegiance, an overwhelming majority of the e-mails were jingoistic knee-jerk responses, such as, "If you can't say the pledge, leave the country"; and "Not everyone owned slaves"; and (especially numerous) "So many people died for our country. The least you can do is pledge to the flag in their honor." As I watched in amazement, I thought about the conflation of liberty with whiteness and how it is related to violence and heroism in war. The fact that freedom and patriotism are so closely aligned in our culture with lockstep conformity and allegiance to victims of war makes it blazingly apparent that liberty is not necessarily considered an individual right, as our pledges and patriotic songs tell us. Liberty is socially determined, and the audience was telling Brooks that she was not free. The not-everyone-owned-slaves response was also telling. Suddenly Brooks's race was an important issue and related to her freedom of speech. As is often the case, when an African American woman speaks, white people mishear her. Brooks was making an important point, especially as a public official, but her statement was buried alive on television in a disorganized free-for-all in which individual pronouncements, such as "Not everyone owned slaves," went unaddressed. This statement was a direct response to Brooks's position and her perfectly legal right to take such a stance. The not-everyone-owned-slaves response is actually used to skirt this country's responsibility for a legacy of slavery that has never really been addressed. Recently, some African American leaders have been pushing for financial compensation for African American descendants of slaves, a perfectly reasonable request and one that Brooks herself has publicly supported. The not-everyone-owned-slaves routine is one way of sidestepping the issue of reparations. Even as modern German and Swiss companies are offering apologies and reparations for Nazi atrocities and the use of human beings in forced labor, Americans wish to continue to bury their heads in the sand and lamely avoid responsibility.

Meanwhile, the American national election of 2000 was scandalously determined in Florida by racist practices, including a completely inaccurate list of supposed felons (many African American) who were not allowed to vote in the presidential election. The *International Herald Tribune* ran an interesting piece (reprinted from the *New York Times*) that described exactly how Republicans used "a private company with close ties to the Republican Party to help 'cleanse' the state's voter registration roles" (Herbert 8); the company, Choice Point, was later forced to acknowledge that eight thousand of the "voters it had listed as felons had in fact been guilty of misdemeanors which would not have affected their right to vote" (8). Even after supposedly correcting the list, Choice Point came up with a "lousy list, riddled with mistakes" (Herbert 8). Marty Fagan, a Choice Point vice president, told Bob Herbert that "there had never been any expectation that the list would be particularly accurate" (8). As Herbert reported, Choice Point eventually came up with "58,000 people—people registered to vote—who would fall into the category of 'possible felons'" (8). African Americans were also turned away from voting booths by various other methods. Meanwhile, I watched as Americans wrote or called CNN on *TalkBack Live* and other programs. The level of racism was utterly jaw-dropping. Many callers and e-mailers called African Americans (and the elderly) "stupid": "If you are too stupid to vote, you shouldn't be in this country." The media played down the Choice Point "felon" list, and even after civil rights activists and the National Association for the Advancement of Colored People (NAACP) came up with compelling and notable examples of race-based voting "irregularities" and outright discrimination, Attorney General John Ashcroft maintains that no such discrimination pattern existed in the 2000 election in Florida. On 6 June 2001, the *New York Times* reported that Governor Jeb Bush of Florida "sent a scathing letter to the United States Commission on Civil Rights . . . denouncing its preliminary findings on the problem-plagued presidential race in Florida" (Canedy 20). But Lois Frankel, a Democrat in the Florida House, said of the commission's report, "Governor Bush is missing the point here. . . . There's something inherently wrong with the system when a black voter is ten times more likely than a white voter to be disenfranchised because of the color of his skin" (20). It is no wonder that Henri Brooks refuses to stand and say the Pledge of Allegiance; in light of recent events, perhaps we should all sit with her.

Similarly, the George W. Bush administration has announced that it finds no race-based discrimination in the application of the death penalty, which is overwhelmingly used against African Americans, Mexican Americans, and other so-called people of color. A study reported in the *New York Times* by Fox Butterfield proved that, indeed, in North Carolina in the 1990s, "the odds of getting a death sentence increased three and a half times if the victim was white rather than black" (10). Numerous studies demonstrate that nonwhites face the death penalty at much higher rates than whites. For example, in the North Carolina study,

> The study examined all 3,990 homicide cases in North Carolina from 1993 to 1997. Of the cases in which a death sentence was possible, 11.6 percent of nonwhite defendants charged with murdering white victims were sentenced to death. In contrast, 6.1 percent of whites charged with murdering whites and 4.7 percent of nonwhites charged with murdering nonwhites received the death penalty. (10)

One interesting conclusion, which says something about the complexity of the death penalty, is that prosecutors seek the death penalty more often in cases involving nonwhite defendants.

> Professor [Jack] Boger said the new study had found that the discrimination in death penalty cases was by prosecutors rather than juries. In fact, he said, what seems to have occurred is not that prosecutors sought the death penalty more often for black defendants but that they were more willing to let defendants plead guilty in exchange for a lesser sentence if the victim was black. (qtd. in Butterfield 10)

Meanwhile, as civilized countries looked on in horror, American officials put to death Timothy McVeigh, who admitted his guilt in murdering 168 people in the infamous 1995 bombing of the Murrah Federal Building in Oklahoma City. The coverage by the American media emphasized that the sanctioned murder of McVeigh would bring "closure" to the relatives of the victims, but on the BBC news, several relatives who witnessed the execution expressed surprise and trauma, saying that the execution brought little closure.

If one believes the American media, many people seem to have a considerable emotional investment in the supposed closure factor provided by McVeigh's death when it applies to victims of the federal building bombing, but these same Americans turn a blind eye to victims of the American holocausts: African Americans and Native Americans. The narrative of the suffering by families of the victims of the Oklahoma City bombing is a narrative with which Americans identify. But the suffering of Africans at the hands of slaveholding Americans is not one that most white Americans are interested in identifying with, and the argument that not every white person owned slaves ignores the fact that, in the larger picture, every white American benefited from the economic gains and power that came of the plantation economy, which relied on the bodies and souls of captured and enslaved Africans.

It is also important to remember that whiteness is not merely a social construction; it is a legal construction as well. Whiteness defined citizenship, freedom; blackness connoted slavery, bondage. Whiteness moved from being just something to be proud of to a legal form of property or, as law scholar Cheryl Harris notes,

> The fact that whiteness is not a "physical" entity does not remove it from the realm of property. . . . Whiteness is not simply and solely a legally recognized property interest. It is simultaneously an aspect of self-identity and of personhood, and its relation to the law of property is complex. Whiteness has functioned as self-identity in the domain of the intrinsic, personal, and psychological; as reputation in the interstices between internal and external identity; and, as property in the extrinsic, public, and legal realms. According whiteness actual legal status converted an aspect of identity into an external object of property, moving whiteness from privileged identity to a vested interest. (104)

It is crucial to note that self-identity in America's race system is driven by circumscribed laws. "The fact of race subordination was coercive and circumscribed the liberty to self-determine," writes Harris, continuing, "Self-determination was not a right for all people, but a privilege accorded on the basis of race" (117). Whiteness became more than just a concept when it became a legal identity marker. According to Harris, "The very fact of citizenship itself was linked to white racial identity. The Naturalization Act of 1790 restricted citizenship to persons who resided in the United States for two years, who could establish their good character in court, and who were 'white'" (117). As Ralph Ellison so eloquently observed, "Since the beginning of the nation, white Americans have suffered from a deep inner uncertainty as to who they really are. One of the ways that has been used to simplify the answer has been to seize upon the presence of black Americans and use them as a marker, a symbol of limits, a metaphor for the 'outsider'" (165–66). In "On Being 'White' . . . and Other Lies," originally published in *Essence* in 1984, James Baldwin emphatically noted that Europeans paid a high price by losing their identity to become white. Germans, Norwegians, Italians, Jews, Poles, and a host of other Europeans became white and guaranteed a future that offered no real sense of community. According to Baldwin,

> America became white—the people who, as they claim, "settled" the country became white—because of the necessity of denying the Black presence, and justifying the Black subjugation. No community can be based on such a principle—or, in other words, no community can be established on so genocidal a lie. (178)

Baldwin concludes that, perversely and ironically, whites "divested themselves of the power to control and *define* themselves" (180) in order to convince themselves that they could control black people, and "in their debasement and definition of black people, they debased and defamed themselves" (180). Similarly, as W. E. B. Du Bois originally wrote in 1920 in "The Souls of White Folk," a chapter in *Darkwater: Voices from within the Veil,*

> It is curious to see America, the United States, looking on herself, first, as a sort of natural peace-maker, then as a moral protagonist in this terrible time. No nation is less fitted for this rôle. . . .
>   Instead of standing as a great example of the success of democracy and the possibility of human brotherhood America has taken her place as an awful example of its pitfalls and failures, so far as black and brown and yellow peoples are concerned. . . . America, Land of Democracy, wanted to believe in the failure of democracy so far as darker peoples were concerned. Absolutely without excuse she established a caste system, rushed into preparation for war, and conquered tropical colonies. She stands today shoulder to shoulder with Europe in Europe's worst sin against civilization. (Du Bois 198)

More than three-quarters of a century later, the administration of George W. Bush is leading us into another cold war, insisting on a new wave of nuclear proliferation with the release of a ridiculous plan for a *Star Wars*-like "weapons shield" that will upset the global power alliance and disregard established anti-ballistic missile treaties. It is as if President Bush and his militarist backers wish to return to the state of white male as sole authority in all social and cultural conflicts. As Trudier Harris explains, white men were performers in the cultural ritual of lynching. The white male's function was to protect his home, especially his property, the white woman; but

> The notion that the white man was really trying to prevent "mongrelization" of the white race is just that—a notion. No such concern for racial purity defined his actions with black women; consequently, his objections to miscegenation were designed to control the behavior of black males and white females without interfering with his own sexual preferences. No one stopped to consider that, during the years of the Civil War, when white men left their wives, daughters, and homes in the hands of black men, not a single instance of rape was reported. The issue, then, really boils down to one between white men and black men and the mythic conception the former have of the latter. (T. Harris 301)

Performing whiteness, then, insists first on identity as "white" and second on performing in the lynching ritual. This played itself out during the execution of Timothy McVeigh. McVeigh, though white, performed his whiteness inaccurately; he aligned himself with white extremists, and he killed almost two hundred people in the bombing of the Oklahoma City federal building. The media went into lynching mode, with morning television shows dedicated to coverage of the event and endless blow-by-blow descriptions of McVeigh's death. McVeigh was marked as other, monster, boogieman, and the American government stepped in, effectively, to lynch him. Ironically, McVeigh identified with what Annalee Newitz and Matthew Wray term "the white victim narrative [which] comes out of 'white power' and holds that affirmative action, immigrants' rights, social welfare programs are racist attacks on whites" (174). The ironies abound here, but I should note that the role the government played in the public execution of McVeigh was race- and class-based and had its roots in America's plantocracy. Attorney General Ashcroft made a surprise appearance at the witness video for victims' families, as if to take credit for the event and to signify his performance as the white male overseer of lynching. Similarly, white male news anchors covered the execution's aftermath in a patronizing fashion meant to support the death penalty and support the false notion that institutionalized murder of the other-beast-murderer will somehow make victims' families achieve so-called closure. On the day of McVeigh's execution, Peter Jennings presented a segment on the *ABC Nightly News* called "Closure," which included a forced moment of silence as audience members watched the mourners weep in anguish at the memorial site of the federal building. The discipline of bodies—the discipline of the authoritative law, supposedly in the name of the people—is what America is about. White America is associated with death and control of bodies, and so is whiteness.

Fear of hybridity fuels whiteness. Whites would not be able to exist were it not for fears of race mixing, gender bending, class-passing, and other forms of hybridity. The white woman as virginal angel is an archetype designed to keep hybridity at bay. As Richard Dyer notes, Lillian Gish and Mary Pickford exemplified a return to the Victorian ideal in the cinema and were "part of a bid for the respectability of the medium" (*White* 127). Similarly, Daniel Bernardi links whiteness to the cinema's bid for respectability: both the Motion Picture Production Code

> and the National Board of Review, supported by industry trades and the critical press, attempted to "upgrade" the actual décor and safety of movie houses as well as "uplift" the audience to a respectable, more bourgeois level. . . . Thus, the move to upgrade and uplift resulted in the narrator system, a bourgeois, patriarchal, white system of narrative integration. (108–9)

One could argue that white female decency was an inherently difficult trope to hold up in Hollywood narrative. Actresses, for one thing, were already associated before the days of vaudeville with a lower-class station and were often aligned with prostitution. But class dissects the issue of respectability in actresses.

> The popular association of actresses and prostitutes is not a straightforward issue of class and gender, for neither actresses nor prostitutes represented a single class of women who uniformly broke specific cultural taboos.
>   The performers singled out as exemplars of the Madonna/whore dichotomy tend to be in the lowest paid and least prestigious specialties

involving the greatest anonymity and impersonalized lines of [the] business. Their low wages, late hours and sexual attractiveness damned them circumstantially, and effective rebuttal was choked. (T. Davis 73)

Even as live performance artists broke cultural taboos outside the arena of theater and film, motion pictures came under attack, especially after the imposition of the Motion Picture Production Code in 1934, for their supposed licentious sexuality, lack of morals, and portrayals of sexual deviance and race mixing. Much has been made of the Code with regard to race, gender, and sexuality, but few have read the Code as a document designed to maintain the borders of whiteness. The Code not only restricted on-screen sexuality but was designed to prohibit various forms of display (and support) of hybridity.

Perhaps no actress is as closely associated with the Motion Picture Production Code as Mae West. I suggest that West not only undermined the Code in terms of her blatant sexuality, but she did so in a variety of other areas by managing to display and support hybridity and transgressive ideas about identity and performativity. The problem is that West's celebrated transgressive identity depended on her return to whiteness and on her displaying herself against a backdrop of black mammies and black gay men. In *I'm No Angel* (1933), for example, West is surrounded by three African American women who play her "maids," often referred to as her "friends" by film critics. The interesting thing is that, in her films, Mae West never has white female friends. Though Doherty writes of West, "[H]er warmest moments are with her maids and girlfriends" (186), in *I'm No Angel,* West, as Tira, treats her black female servants as both slaves and confidantes with whom she shares sexual remarks about men. One could even argue that West commodifies and appropriates blackness for its supposed sexuality, humor, and musicality in her strange performance in the film that at once appropriates male sexual desire, black female humor, and openness about sexuality and blues numbers co-opted from black women, such as Bessie Smith. Mae West is celebrated for her transgressive performances of drag, but exactly who or what is she dragging? She burlesques white upper-class women, through her clothes and jewelry; lower-class white women, in her language and station as a circus performer; and white men, for their sexual come-ons. She is also herself in drag, with her overly exaggerated hip-bouncing gate, almost like a female John Wayne. And yet she borrows from black women and black

FIGURE 4. Mae West and Cary Grant in a classic pose of heterocentric whiteness in *I'm No Angel* (1933). Courtesy Jerry Ohlinger Archives.

gay men, whom she also drags through body language and appropriation of language and song. She drags the black mammy figures around her as well, much in the manner of Sophie Tucker. She's also playing, more obviously, a drag routine in her central role as a floozy lion tamer and lady hustler. She may be no angel, but she's a multigendered, multiraced, multiclassed, transmogrified constitution of polyvalent drag acts all rolled into one dangerous, threatening white woman. Yet for all of her performances of hybridity and transgressiveness, as Doherty points out, "West was no fallen woman, not even a bad girl" (186). That Mae West could manage to upset the censors is perhaps a tribute to her polyvalence as drag artist. I think she was most upsetting because she performed all this hybridity and drag in a white female body, but she did so very much at the expense of blackness, especially black femaleness.

The black women in *I'm No Angel* are fascinating in light of Mae West's threat of hybridity. In the film West plays Tira, a lion tamer who uses men for sexual gratification and expensive gifts, but she loses her power and sense of threat when she falls for Jack Clayton (Cary Grant). Before meeting Clayton, Tira's favorite saying with regard to men had been "find 'em, fool 'em, and forget 'em," but along the way she is aided and supported by three black maids, Beulah, Libby, and an unnamed woman (played by Gertrude Howard, Libby Taylor, and Hattie McDaniel, respectively). Many critics note and quote her outrageous sexual come-ons, but no one seems to address the problematic nature of her slave-friend relationships with African American women in the film. Sometimes the McDaniel, Taylor, and Howard characters act merely as witnesses to Tira's outrageous behavior; yet sometimes one wonders if West is appropriating the black sexuality, humor, and suggestive blues numbers from the black women with whom she surrounds herself. Indeed, many of Tira's wisecracks are underscored by friendly laughter on the part of her maids. One has to ask if West is performing *for* the black actresses, who play Tira's only women friends and whom she sometimes treats like slaves. At one point in the narrative, Tira is asked to spice up her lion-tamer routine by placing her head in the jaws of the lion. She does so, wearing a glowing white sequined bodice and carrying a whip in her hand. Afterward we see her with Beulah, to whom she confides, "Well, Beulah, that's another performance under my belt. When I was born with this face it was the same as striking oil." Gertrude Howard, as Beulah, throws back her head and performs a hearty, full-throated laugh and underscores Tira's statements with utterances such as "uh huh," "you said it," and the like. But because of class difference, and because of her unwillingness to perform appropriately as a virginal white woman, Tira is othered by a party of upper-class whites who come to visit her backstage. She doesn't get along with these "silk-hat" types, as she makes clear to her black maids. Later we witness a jaw-dropping montage in which all three black women are shown giving Tira a manicure, pedicure, and hairdo. She is preparing for a big date, and one of her maids, Libby, says to her, "I been under the impression that you is a one-man woman," to which Tira responds, "I am. One man at a time." All three black mammy figures make it clear that they are most impressed by Tira's ability to seduce and attract men. The relationship seems friendly and very much conspiratorial, yet when Tira is angry at one of the silk-hat white women, she says—memorably—to Beulah, "Oh, Beulah . . . peel me a grape," demonstrating that theirs is a master-servant relationship subject to its attendant abuses and familiarities.

Perhaps West sought to be associated with blackness because, as Frantz Fanon notes, "[T]he Negro represents the sexual instinct in its raw state. The Negro is the incarnation of a genital potency beyond all moralities and prohibitions . . . the keeper of the impalpable gate that opens into the realm of orgies, of bacchanals, of delirious sexual sensations" (177). Mae West's appropriation of blackness reminds me of bell hooks's writings about pop star Madonna. White privilege, hooks maintains, allows Madonna to imitate black pleasure without understanding the complexity of black pain. "And it is no wonder then that when [whites] attempt to imitate the joy in living which they see as the 'essence' of soul and blackness, their cultural productions may have an air of sham and falseness that may titillate and even move white audiences yet leave many black folks cold" (*Black* 158). Perhaps Mae West, like Madonna, can be accused of commodifying race as, in bell hooks's words, "an alternative playground where members of dominating races, genders, sexual practices affirm their power-over in intimate relations with the Other" (23). Before we celebrate the subversiveness of Mae West's drag and gender-blending act, we must certainly take into account her power as a white woman. If, as hooks notes, "the socially constructed image of innocent white womanhood relies on the continued production of the racist/sexist sexual myth that black women are not innocent and never can be" (160), then what do we do with West's

38

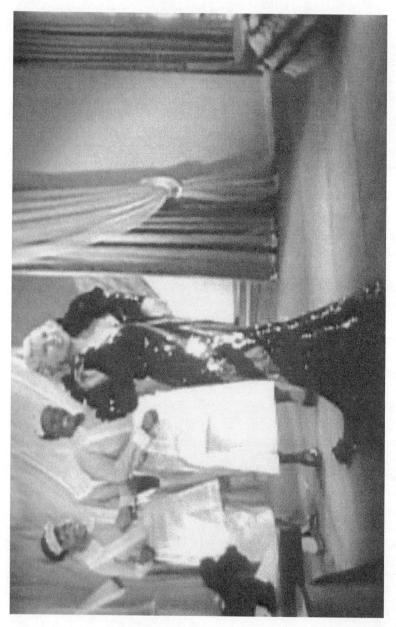

FIGURE 5. Mae West appropriates performative blackness in *I'm No Angel* (1933). Courtesy Jerry Ohlinger Archives.

socially constructed image of white womanhood in defiance of inno-
cence? Does Mae West perhaps underscore the fragility of female whiteness itself as a construct? In a racist and sexist society, after all, white
women are a problem. Philosopher Lewis Gordon urges us to rethink
our notions of the white woman.

> She stands as a white blackness, as a living contradiction of white supremacy.
> Out of her comes every white, placing a question mark on the notion of the
> purity of whiteness in the flesh. Unlike the black woman, out of whom only
> black children can be born, she can bear *both* white and black children.
> Because of this, the white woman ultimately stands on the same ontological
> level as slime in an antiblack world. She is regarded as a frightening sub-
> stance that simultaneously attracts and repels. (305)

Perhaps in *I'm No Angel*, Mae West is performing "a white blackness" or
"a question mark," and maybe surrounding herself with black femaleness
was one way of performing a site of contestation against stereotypes about
white and black women. Even though the black mammy figure buttresses
the sexual transgressiveness of such white female performers as Mae West,
Jean Harlow, Barbara Stanwyck, and Marlene Dietrich, it does not necessarily follow that black women are simply defeminized or reduced to signifier status.

> The common plaint that black women in film are frequently "defeminized"
> may imply that they become "simply" a racial signifier. As Hortense
> Spillers, bell hooks, and others have emphasized, dominant constructions
> of black femininity are indeed not "feminized" after the white model. Such
> stereotypes are not simply "inaccurate" but select and freeze differences
> operative and enforced in society. One of the primary ways black women
> characters bear the weight of sexual ideology is in their relationship of con-
> trast with white heroines. Some elements of this distinctive gendering of
> black women in dominant texts may be keyed to lesbian stereotypes. Thus
> what is perhaps intended to disempower and "other" black women all the
> more—and often succeeds, in a consumer culture that valorizes white het-
> erosexual femininity—can be read for other meanings, as a site of contesta-
> tion. (White 152)

Contestation of the norms of white heterosexual femininity is what
Mae West is celebrated for; however, if it comes on the back of black

femininity, it is clearly problematic. This is especially true in light of the fact that visibility of white women is connected to suppression of black bodies and the rise of white women as consumers in American culture. For, as Siobhan B. Somerville notes,

> The new visibility of white women in movie audiences, I suggest, was connected to the suppression of visibly black bodies both on the screen and in the audience. Audiences' "fear of the dark" at movie theaters was both literal and figurative. Racial segregation acted as an imagined defense against the powerful myth of black men's sexual threat to white women. According to the logic of Jim Crow, white women could circulate more securely in racially homogeneous social spaces. The increasing control over the mobility of African American men and women coincided with white women being encouraged to circulate as consumers within the commodity culture. (68–69)

West manifests her power as a consumer, displaying furs, jewels, stockings, negligees, and numerous gifts and acquisitions that she discards as easily as she discards men. Men are accessories in Tira's life, and they are represented by a number of figurines, such as a dog, a rat, a lamb, next to the photograph of each disregarded man to act as reminders of Tira's sexual conquests. Sexuality and the power of sexual conquest are not only associated with blackness but with white maleness. Indeed, Jeanine Basinger calls West a male aggressor who "combined the idea of woman as submissive sex partner with the idea of woman playing male aggressor. . . . Her image, highly complex and self-contradictory, was that of a woman freely acting like a man" (181). But Mae West is frequently seen as a gay male in drag in a woman's body. Her gender bending is famous. In 1926 she produced a play called *The Drag,* with an all-male, all-gay cast. Police closed the play, and West was briefly jailed. She asked the New York police to stop beating up homosexuals, according to Vito Russo, who quotes her as stating, "[A] homosexual is a female soul in a male body. You're hitting a woman, I says" (55). It stands to reason that West may have believed she was a male soul performing in a female body. West's performances of the white female body remain enigmatic and potentially subversive, but transgression does not necessarily mandate an undertaking of *racial* subversion. West's performance and relation *to* race remains limited *by* race in part because, as Ruth Frankenberg states,

Whiteness changes over time and space and is in no way a transhistorical essence. . . . Thus, the range of possible ways of living whiteness, for an individual white woman in a particular time and place, is delimited by the relations of racism *at that moment and in that place.* And if whiteness varies spatially and temporally, it is also a relational category, one that is constructed with a range of other racial and cultural categories, with class and with gender. (*White Women* 236)

The moment and place of the staging of whiteness in the case of Mae West was under the noses of the censors of the Motion Picture Production Code of the late 1930s. Regardless of what we make of West's drag routine and her seeming kinship with black mammy types, West needs to be credited for attempting to disrupt the cultural norms of her day. West's white female is a hybrid. Yes, she has power and, yes, she gets her man in the end, but she is also buried under falseness and utter fabrication. Her hair is an unnaturally white blond; her body is deformed by tight bodices designed to force her white breasts up into the viewer's nose; her face is painted almost beyond recognition; she speaks in a suggestive, almost inaudible moan. She breaks out into song and becomes, at times, a performative, female, white-dragging-black blues singer, with such numbers as "I Want You, I Need You" and "Sister Honky Tonk." She's a hybrid threat to white women. "A better dame than you once called me a liar and they had to sew her up in twelve different places," Tira says to Alicia (Gertrude Michael), a white, refined, silk-hat type. One cannot help but celebrate her outrageous sexual aggression in a time when white women were straitjacketed by proscriptions for proper behavior. In response to the outrage and criticism she received after the release of *I'm No Angel,* West was unrepentant. As recounted by Doherty, "'Yes,' she admitted, 'I wrote the story of *I'm No Angel* myself. It's all about a girl who lost her reputation and never missed it.' When asked what she thought of the censors, West wisecracked, 'Tell them they made me what I am today. I hope they're satisfied'" (187). If being white was defined as being respectable, Mae West as a white woman displayed the ineffectiveness of such a definition. Her borrowings from black female culture (not to mention gay male culture) are perhaps key to understanding her hybrid status.

One example of such a relationship comes in the celebrated pre-Code film *Baby Face* (1933), which featured Barbara Stanwyck as Lily Powers and Theresa Harris as Chico, Lily's maid, friend, and (perhaps) lover. In *Baby Face* Stanwyck plays a hardened woman who grew up in the slums.

Lily is forced by her own father, who runs a speakeasy, to serve beer and turn tricks for the customers. After her father's death, Lily flees her hometown of Erie, Pennsylvania, and ends up in New York City. No matter how poor and down on her luck, she remains faithful only to her black maid. Their relationship is unusual. They share a closeness that sometimes makes the viewer wonder if they are sexual companions. Lily's attitude toward men is informed by her horrible and downtrodden background. She is fueled by hatred for men. In her last fight with her father, who calls her a tramp, Lily responds, "Yeah, I'm a tramp and who's to blame? My father! A swell start you gave me. Nothin' but dirty men! Dirty, rotten men, and you're rottener than any of 'em. I'll hate you as long as I live!"

In New York Lily finds her way to a job in a skyscraper. She literally moves her way up in the world by using men, and we see her rise in a series of shots of the exterior of the building. Each time she moves up, the camera cuts to a shot of the skyscraper and we hear a blues song on the soundtrack. The song is "St. Louis Woman," a tragic blues number often sung by Chico. Lily manipulates white men in much the same manner Tira does in *I'm No Angel*, but both eventually fall in love and marry one particular man. In *Baby Face* Lily falls for Courtland Trenholm (George Brent), the president of the Gotham Trust Co. The two have a whirlwind romance, and Lily shows Chico a bag full of jewels, cash, stocks, and bonds that she has accrued through the relationship. Suddenly, Trenholm's bank fails and he needs the money he gave to Lily, but Lily will not part with it; she leaves with Chico on a ship bound for Europe. At the last minute, before the ship sails, Lily races back to Trenholm, only to find that, in despair, Trenholm has attempted suicide. Trenholm is nevertheless revived by Lily's love. Lily hands over the money, and the couple live happily ever after in a state of white heterotopia. Lily certainly depicts a hybrid fantasy of white femaleness. The message of the film, as summarized by Doherty, is that "a determined female sexual predator can break down the resistance of any male no matter how outwardly moral his exterior" (132).

But more interesting than Lily's relationship with Trenholm is her relationship with Chico. Is the African American female here a stand-in for the white female's conscience? So many times throughout the film, Chico launches into singing "St. Louis Woman," the traditional black blues ballad of a woman "with her diamond rings" who meets a bad fate, and at one point Lily begs her maid not to sing the song. It's as if they both know that Lily, as a white woman, is performing the ballad of the St. Louis woman, a black woman's story of suffering, and the absurdity of it is that Lily is white but incorrectly performing her whiteness. Chico acts as a motherly companion to Lily, and, as Patricia White notes, "African American women mothering white women represents a particularly loaded relationship" (156). The intimacy between the women of different races is certainly open to consideration. Chico and Lily share mutually charged looks in close-up, for example, and Lily often tells Chico her secrets. Chico gives advice and council, either outright or in the form of singing "St. Louis Woman" as a commentary on Lily's life. Here, though, "the black woman is not merely an echo" (153); she is a spiritual guide and moral compass. It is clear that each woman would not be able to survive without the other. Chico aids Lily's corporate rise and remarks on Lily's ability to conquer men. Yet theirs is a hierarchical relationship that is dependent on and defined by white patriarchal hegemony. This relationship is common in Hollywood fantasies of female friendships that cut across racial lines.

Mildred Pierce (1945), for example, features an uncredited Butterfly McQueen as Lottie, a maid, and Joan Crawford as Mildred Pierce. Here McQueen's character acts as a mere servant in Mildred's ambitious plan to build an empire of restaurants throughout southern California. In the beginning of the film Lottie is seen in the kitchen of Mildred's modest house doing the *really* dirty work. While Mildred's daughter, Veda (Ann Blyth), complains that her mother is demeaning herself by doing such menial labor as baking pies, it is really Lottie who is the slave in the kitchen, scrubbing pans and baking racks while Mildred's apron seems barely smudged. Once again, it is the figure of the black woman behind the constructed white matriarch who does the lion's share of the actual labor and gets no credit for it, beyond a meager salary. In addition, McQueen's childlike demeanor throughout the film (honed to perfection in 1939's *Gone with the Wind*) makes her seem more a dependent than a coequal, or even a coequal laborer.

Clearly, on-screen representation of the relationships between white women and their African American maids differs in *Mildred Pierce*. In *Baby Face* and *I'm No Angel* the relationship between the white female lead character and the black maid is suffused with an intimacy lacking in that of *Mildred Pierce*. Mae West, as Tira, shares confidences with her maids.

44

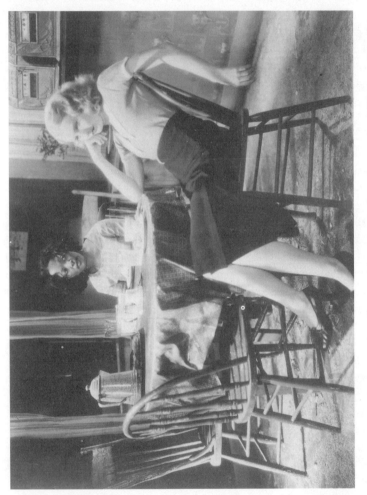

FIGURE 6. Problematic sisterhood enacted between Barbara Stanwyck and Theresa Harris in *Baby Face* (1933). Courtesy Museum of Modern Art Stills Archive.

FIGURE 7. Butterfly McQueen watches from the background *(left)* as Joan Crawford performs upwardly mobile female whiteness in *Mildred Pierce* (1945), with Jack Carson *(center)*. Courtesy Jerry Ohlinger Archives.

Similarly, Barbara Stanwyck, as Lily, shares secrets with Theresa Harris, as Chico. These examples of films from the 1930s differ dramatically from *Mildred Pierce*. Joan Crawford, as Mildred, is contrasted against Butterfly McQueen, as Lottie, who is portrayed as a purely menial figure. The plots differ as well, with Depression-era films pitting women against men and thus allowing for more transgression along race lines. In *Mildred Pierce* Mildred is in sexual competition with her daughter, who treats Lottie with scorn and destroys any possibility of friendship between her mother and her maid. As African Americans fought for their rights in the post-World War II era, Hollywood, fearing the cataclysmic social change this fight would bring, responded by relegating blacks to ever more stereotyped, marginalized on-screen roles. Clearly, the complexities of black-white relationships between women in the cinema are, as Patricia White suggests, "particularly loaded" and constitute an area of investigation for future scholars.

CHAPTER THREE

WHITE FACE, WHITE SPACE

Much has been written about blackface and race stereotypes in American cinema. Though such study reveals the politics of minstrelsy, a consideration of white stereotyping exposes the political ramifications and practice of performing whiteness in a form of ethnic passing that may be called *whiteface*. The reasons behind the widespread phenomenon of blackface are well known, but the practice of whiteface deserves consideration, identification, and definition. While blackface involves makeup (usually burnt cork), whiteface involves performing whiteness in such a way that traces of ethnicity are erased. Whiteface defines the cinematic landscape as a white space. Blackface made for a safe place for black minstrelsy within white cinematic space. As Michael Rogin accurately asserts, "Slavery forced Africans to perform for whites; the truth behind the fantasy that blackface accurately represented plantation slaves was that it mimed their expropriation. By domesticating transgressive desire, servitude made blacks safe for white attraction" (22). The popularity of blackface was so commonplace that "Disney's white-gloved and black-faced Mickey Mouse was copied from *The Jazz Singer*" (29). Minstrelsy continues to be part of the fabric of the dominant, often racist, white American culture that is reigned over by the Mouse and his progeny, even today. In fact, one could argue that little has been done to address blackface, at least in the public eye and in the mass consumption of minstrelsy and blackface in American film culture, other than the production of Spike Lee's typically transgressive film, *Bamboozled* (2000). *The Jazz Singer* (1927) regularly plays on television in reruns and is unproblematically hailed as the first successful sound picture. The sight of Al Jolson in blackface—eyes popped, lips whitened, on one knee and singing "Mammy"—is not really questioned outside academe. Academe has done a masterful job, in fact, of providing legitimacy to the resoundingly racist *Birth of a Nation* (1915), a film that is still celebrated by film buffs and film critics, some of whom even today make excuses for the film's overwhelming racism. *Birth of a Nation* supports the actions of the Ku Klux Klan (KKK) and portrays black men as rapists of white women. Many still think that *Gone with the Wind* is the greatest film ever made, never stopping to consider the racism of the film. When the NAACP made objections during filming of *Gone with the Wind,* according to Rogin, David O. Selznick "insisted that he had 'cleaned up' Margaret Mitchell's Pulitzer Prize-winning novel[;] . . . the black men who assault Scarlett O'Hara in the novel metamorphose in the film . . . into dirty, lower-class, white trash" (164). A black man tries to save Scarlett and she is also given a safe black mammy, played by Hattie McDaniel. That McDaniel won an Academy Award for best supporting actress underscores white Americans' desire for comforting roles of on-screen blacks. Blackface shows up regularly in classic Hollywood films, such as the Bing Crosby vehicle *Holiday Inn* (1942), famous for the introduction of the smash Christmas song "White Christmas." Race difference and race cognizance are erased by the white supremacy of *Holiday Inn,* underscoring Ruth Frankenberg's remarks about the dangers of viewing "white culture" as normative.

> There are a number of dangers inherent in continuing to view white culture as no culture. Whiteness appeared in the narratives to function as both norm or core, that against which everything else is measured, and as residue, that which is left after everything else has been named. A far-reaching danger of whiteness coded as "no culture" is that it leaves in place whiteness as defining a set of normative cultural practices against which all are measured and into which all are expected to fit. (*White Women* 204)

Goodness, pleasure, the sanctity of Christmas—all are associated with whiteness in *Holiday Inn,* and in so many other Hollywood fantasies.

Even in the 1930 Production Code, reprinted in *Pre-Code Hollywood,* it is clear that goodness is linked to whiteness, the human race is defined as white, and the only element of whiteness that is undesirable or dangerous is class difference. The lone reference to race comes in the discussion of sex and how it should be presented: "MISCEGENATION (sex relationship between the white and black races) is forbidden" (qtd. in

Doherty 363), and the only mention that smacks of ethnicity comes in an addendum to the Code called "National feelings," wherein "The history, institutions, prominent people and citizenry of other nations should be represented fairly" (364). But it is the beginning of the Code that speaks to the issue of whiteness by *not* speaking to the issue of whiteness and by using the terms *human beings* and *human race,* which are clearly understood to mean white.

FIRST SECTION
GENERAL PRINCIPLES

I. Theatrical motion pictures, that is, pictures intended for the theatre as distinct from pictures intended for churches, schools, lecture halls, educational movements, social reform movements, etc., are primarily to be regarded as *Entertainment.*

Mankind has always recognized the importance of entertainment and its value in rebuilding the bodies and souls of human beings.

But it has always recognized that entertainment can be of a character either *helpful* or *harmful* to the human race, and, in consequence, has clearly distinguished between:

Entertainment which tends to improve the race, or, at least, to recreate and rebuild human beings exhausted with the realities of life; and *Entertainment which tends to degrade human beings,* or to lower their standards of life and living.

Hence the *moral importance* of entertainment is something which has been universally recognized. It enters intimately into the lives of men and women and affects them closely; it occupies their minds and affections during leisure hours, and ultimately touches the whole of their lives. A man may be judged by his standard of entertainment as easily as by the standard of his work.

So *correct entertainment raises* the whole standard of a nation.

Wrong entertainment lowers the whole living condition and moral ideals of a race. (347–48)

The Code emphasizes the moral obligations of the art of motion pictures, and class difference in audiences makes film art problematic for the censor. The widespread appeal to the masses and the multitudes of white people, who are wearing different ethnicities, different classes, wearing *difference* itself, is emphatically problematic. "Certain classes" are addressed later in the Code.

III. The motion picture has special *Moral obligations:*

(A) Most arts appeal to the mature. This art appeals at once *to every class*—mature, immature, developed, undeveloped, law-abiding, criminal. Music has its grades for different classes; so has literature and drama. This art of the motion picture, combining as it does the two fundamental appeals of looking at a picture and listening to a story, at once reaches every class of society.

(B) Because of the mobility of a film and the ease of picture distribution, and because of the possibility of duplicating positives in large quantities, this art *reaches places* unpenetrated by other forms of art.

(C) Because of these two facts, it is difficult to produce films intended for only *certain classes of people.* The exhibitor's theatres are built for the masses, for the cultivated and the rude, mature and immature, self-restrained and inflammatory, young and old, law-respecting and criminal. Films, unlike books and music, can with difficulty be confined to certain selected groups. (qtd. in Doherty 349)

The subtext of this narrative betrays discomfort with regard to differences in class and ethnicity. There is a fear of the uncontrollable nature of motion pictures and their audiences. I suspect that this fear has to do with an unspoken understanding that motion pictures should be a space to deploy whiteness and to flatten out class difference. It is as if the framers of the Code well understood that, as audience members, the supposed uncultivated, rude masses coproduce the images they watch, and no matter how "moral" or "white" (here practically interchangeable ideas), the audience brought a heterogeneity to viewership that clearly disconcerted the censors. This brings up the slippery slope of white performativity and the white public space necessary to deploy whiteness. The nature of white space is uncanny: it is a space both open and closed, both inclusive and exclusive. Patricia McKee calls for a postmodern definition of white space.

If white persons project certain kinds of otherness beyond the bounds of whiteness, they also project a wide range of both similarities and differences into public exchange *as* parts of whiteness. Identities of whiteness are in circulation, one might say, in the space between any individual white person and the irremediably "other," massed identity of blackness.

. . . [I]n the more visual terms of twentieth-century public life, there is a wide range of images of whiteness. White persons, therefore, can experience their identity not merely as self-same but as diverse. (McKee 13–14)

I suggest that this white space, where exchanges of identity are nego-tiated, is the space of whiteface, where class and ethnicity are homoge-nized, sterilized, and largely erased in motion pictures. In other words, when I use the term *whiteface,* I do not mean the opposite of blackface. I regard whiteface as a space where representation that demands class-pass-ing, class othering, giving up ethnic identity to become white, and insists that the human race, especially in America, is white. In short, most motion pictures are spaces of whiteface. Whiteface is about space owner-ship and identity claims. It is therefore possible that whites become their own other in whiteface and that whites carry their own burden of repre-sentation, which is the burden of representing that which does not really exist, that which has come to be known as *whiteness.* Perhaps it could also be argued that whites share with blacks a split, or double, identity. White-face demands that class markers and ethnic markers be erased. Last names must be changed to sound more Anglo-Saxon, accents and marks of lower- or working-class origin must be either erased or seen as clearly other. Perceptions of whiteness are dependent, then, on the mask of whiteface. One must give up all claims of ethnicity to be properly white; thus we have a record of ethnic othering and ethnic passing to match no other in Hollywood history. Similarly, whites are forced to take up class-passing in their mastery of whiteface. White actors are regularly asked to lose accents that are related to working-class identity, and they attend act-ing school to learn how to perform whiteness. All this white fakery is in support of a biological fantasy because white as a race does not exist. But in America we insist that a white race does exist. This accounts for wide-spread performances of white minstrelsy.

In film actors perform whiteness against a backdrop of white space and white music. Hollywood music may be defined as white: it *becomes* clearly other only *to* other, and it does so only when an ethnicity is oth-ered as a stereotype. For example, when Asian characters (whether they be Chinese, Japanese, or Malaysian) enter a film or cartoon, there is often a signature musical theme that *underscores* the characters' difference. Cer-tain eight-bar themes are universally used throughout films and cartoons to represent (and to other) the representatives of "the Orient." Native Americans often are introduced by a musical motif of drums, the "*dum*-dum-dum-dum, *dum*-dum-dum-dum" theme, which is the universal aural iconic expression for "Indian." Africans in jungle-adventure films are underscored with drumbeats. A few beats of a rumba often introduce a Latin American character. African Americans often get a brief bar of blues, jazz, or spiritual on the soundtrack to connote American blackness. Italians are scored with a handful of easily recognizable themes. Irish and Scots are othered by a hybrid sort of jig or by a few bars from "Danny Boy" or "When Irish Eyes Are Smiling." Russians and Slavs are signified by "The Volga Boatmen." Swedes and Hollanders are marked by northern European folk tunes on the soundtrack. A few bars suffice to introduce the comfort or threat of the other. In the same fashion that a French citizen is accompanied by a few notes on an accordion upon first cinematic entrance, the eponymous monster in John Carpenter's version of *The Thing* (1982) is introduced with a repetitive motif of synthesized minor chords. Otherness is frequently attended by sound and music, and here ethnicity is equated with otherness. Monster or Irishman, E.T. or Slav, Glinda the Good Witch, or "China-man," each has a musical trope. In view of this musical marking, it is obvious that only the whitest "norm," the Anglo-Saxon, lacks any musical marking or cue. Whiteness that is not marked by ethnicity or class is *not* seen as other. Despite assuming a character is white without being told, it takes an enormous amount of performative work to negotiate whiteface, and the effort must remain perpetually ongoing, for it will collapse if not constantly reinforced and maintained.

Concomitantly, celluloid efforts to suppress hybrid forms of whiteness are perhaps matched only by American immigrants' attempts to forge new identities in an alien land. Whiteface is expected of immigrants, both on- and off-screen. Charles Musser's work about comedy and ethnicity sheds light on this point.

First, immigrants had to cope with the difficult task of forging new identities that matched their new environment. Although some found it possible to exist within the confines of their own ethnic neighborhoods, more typically they had to master a new language, as well as customs and mores. Most took new kinds of jobs. The immigrant was compelled, in short, to become someone else—to become . . . an Other. This meant playing a role—hiding, denying, obscuring, even shedding earlier held, and deeply engrained, identities. It was typically alienating and seemingly unremitting. It also raised crucial questions that put the immigrant on the defensive. Was the self presented to the outside world a "real self" or a false one? And if it was false, was this mask malicious? Would this new self last or would it be discarded like an old suit of clothes? The native-born were never quite sure. Immigrants might change their names, lose their accents, and vote Republican, but their inevitable need to negotiate between two cultures made their allegiance suspect. It was this very fact of role-playing that became part of cinema's core. (42)

The star system demanded whiteface and white minstrelsy. Actors, unless specifically hired to play an ethnic type or a class type, were expected to maintain whiteness by appearing to be homogenized, white, and American. To fully look and perform as white American, all aspects of ethnicity were to be erased. Ian C. Jarvie, in his fascinating study of stars and ethnicity, refers to the homogenizing effect of Hollywood. "Hollywood participated in the process of assimilating Americans of diverse origin, not by enforcing Norman Rockwell life-styles at home but rather by projecting and promoting a picture of American culture and society more homogenized than true" (96).

Perceptions of whiteness are not simply subject to homogenizing whiteface performance. They are also coproduced by audiences. Given that American audiences are heterogeneous it seems that whiteness can be shared by the viewer, regardless of the ethnicity or class of the performer or the audience member. If whiteness can be shared and participated in, desired and facilitated, the question remains: Can white subjectivity be a shared experience coproduced and coexperienced by all audiences? How much of our perception of whiteness is informed by the relationship between actor and viewer?

The performance and reception of whiteface allows for a postmodern model wherein fluid subject positions allow actors and audiences to be "both subjects and objects of view."

Individuals can see themselves, or parts of themselves, in these images and signs; others, at least in part, are also represented. This space of circulating signs and images is more important to the unity of a group than is any bounded structure, because the unity of the group lies not in containment but in the open expression of similarities and differences by the individuals in the group. This representation of similarity and difference provides the group with cohesion and diversity. The communal or racial identity provided by these means is one that allows, even encourages, the expression of difference within the group.

The convertibility of positions among such persons means that they are both subjects and objects of view. (McKee 15)

Thus an immutable, stable identity of whiteness would seem impossible to construct and maintain. This might explain why Hollywood and its audiences desperately attempt to maintain whiteness in the face of its inherent mutability.

A good case in point is a silent film that directly addresses ethnicity, whiteness, and, especially in its title, Americanness. This early short film, *Making an American Citizen* (1912), directed by Alice Guy Blaché, herself a French immigrant to America, explores the whitening of an immigrant Russian couple who arrive in the United States unprepared to become white and American. The film is fascinating in retrospect because of its blatant examination of what it is to be white and American. The film exemplifies and instructs the viewer in the making and performing of whiteness. Because of his ethnicity, Ivan Orloff (Lee Beggs), the ethnic type, is viewed as a bearer of social illness, improper behavior, and an offense to proper white American male behavior. Interestingly enough, Blaché codes proper white male behavior through a feminist lens. But her feminism is decidedly problematic in terms of race. In America becoming a good-white husband entails relearning everyday performance and performing American whiteness. Performing whiteness properly is the main lesson learned by the immigrant couple.

In the opening shot we see Ivan behaving as a spousal abuser, whipping his unnamed wife (Blanch Cornwall) immediately after they arrive in America, treating her as chattel, as she pulls the cart holding her husband and the couple's belongings. His Russian friends do nothing to intervene on her behalf. His friends wear rags and excessive facial hair (hair is sometimes linked to the bestial nature of ethnicity, and ethnicity is coded here as animal-like). Unlike the unkempt Russians, a "white" intervenes (thus whiteness is coded as civility). This white male is clearly upper class, and he performs his whiteness so well that his ethnicity is indeterminate. He is no longer a performer of hybridity. He is completely Americanized and white. Throughout the film, freedom is associated with whiteness and tied to proper marital behavior. Ivan is taught to perform whiteness properly. Likewise, Ivan's wife is taught to perform female whiteness. The series of "lessons in Americanism" may be read as "lessons in whiteness" as much as they are lessons in Blaché's version of feminism.

In the next scene Ivan's spousal abuse is met with scorn by a better performer of whiteness, presumably an Irish American who has learned to rid himself of most of his own ethnicity. Though later in the film whiteness is also associated with the penal system, here white is performed as might. The stock Irish character uses fisticuffs to "teach" Ivan to perform as white. He beats up Ivan and tells him not to beat his wife.

The third lesson involves whiteness and the division of labor between the sexes. The primacy of the private sphere is established as a location of civilizing whiteness reigned over by a proper white "angel of the house." We see the woman correctly performing white femininity by keeping a nice home and gardening. When she asks her husband to help, he is unhelpful and obstinate. Another white ethnic type, coded as German or Amish, perhaps even Quaker, intervenes in the couple's dispute over physical labor, whipping Ivan to teach him proper behavior. As Ivan's wife is seen as being unable to defend herself, white femininity is also equated with frailty. It is interesting to note here the contrast between the wife who could earlier pull a carriage like a beast of burden and the later fainting spell by the same woman.

When a title card reads "Ivan's wife begins to live in the American way," she is properly doing whiteness by smoothly running her home. She has bought a tablecloth and has obviously made efforts at domesticating both her husband and herself. But Ivan has still not been made into a white American citizen. He is still prone to laziness and violence against women. A couple of men overhear a domestic dispute between the couple and intervene. In this somewhat fantastical version of white American justice, Blaché presents the viewer with a white view of a feminist utopia. Not only do white men stand up for women's rights here, but the law also supports her in her quest for justice in the film. One of the most interesting, if rather long, sequences in the film is the courtroom scene. Presided over by a white-haired, white-bearded judge, the proceedings are largely attended by bearded men, white men listening to the evidence of spousal abuse. The lone female figure barely gets a chance to speak, but Ivan spends a fair amount of time defending himself. Is he on trial for performing whiteness poorly or for performing domestic abuse? He is on trial for improper behavior as a white American; as the titles tell us, he has yet to become "completely Americanized."

I suggest that Blaché is speaking through a dialogism here. While the film would ostensibly be about Americanization, it is actually an interesting hybrid of a feminist polemic with the rhetoric of whiteness—a rhetoric erasing ethnicity while at the same time being a springboard for a feminist polemic and a utopian desire for women's rights.

The lawmakers side with Ivan's wife, and he is sent to prison. The vision of Ivan on the chain gang evokes the signifier of prison as a whitener—which is still with us in America today—prison defined as a place for the supposed schooling in proper (read *white*) behavior. Interestingly, the message of *Making an American Citizen* is that only after imprisonment is Ivan properly Americanized.

After Ivan's return from prison, the vision of Ivan's wife, dressed in white, ringing a bell to call her now docile, decent husband, belittles him as an ethnic type and codes him as slightly effeminate. He is shown obediently carrying a basket and watermelon for his wife and putting on a dinner jacket. Whiteness is here associated with properly performing class and also religious piety (the couple are seen praying for the first time). Thus to be properly American is to be pious and religious, solicitous to your wife. *Making an American Citizen* is an unformulaic film that contains uneasy, multivalent messages. It is an early white feminist tract, but it makes its feminist statements on the basis of white privilege and the othering of ethnicity. It is not easy to categorize, celebrate, or dismiss.

Making an American Citizen is not the only example of Alice Guy Blaché's films to push for the rights of women while degrading nonwhites. Her version of the life of Christ, *La Vie du Christ* (1906), is similarly imbalanced in its treatment of women and nonwhites. African bodies (black bodies) are clearly the villains in the film, while white women and children are prominently seen aiding, helping, and guiding Christ. Blacks take part in the scourging and beating of Christ and hold the cross that he is nailed to. Clearly, for Blaché, performing whiteness is associated with goodness and the "frail sex," while performing blackness is associated with evil and otherness.

Among the numerous works that Blaché directed during her early years, *La Vie du Christ* was one of her major accomplishments. The film was an ambitious spectacle that used lavish budgets, large crews, and hundreds of extras in settings designed and executed by Henri Menessier. Blaché skillfully managed to incorporate scores of extras to give added depth to her work, the same way that the American director D. W. Griffith did a decade later in *Birth of a Nation* and *Intolerance* (1916). Indeed, for its period, *La Vie du Christ* is an exceptionally lavish production. Blaché spared no expense to bring her vision to the screen.

La Vie du Christ was released in Paris in April 1906 and was subsequently released with translated intertitles in May 1907 in the United

States. It is divided into twenty-five separate scenes, from the arrival in Bethlehem, in which Joseph and Mary are turned away from the stable, to the burial of Christ. By the standards of the period, *La Vie du Christ* is both ambitious and lavish in production, as well as epic in running time: twenty-five minutes in an era in which most films lasted only a few minutes. In each of the sequences of the film, Blaché formalizes and ritualizes the life and death of Christ as a series of performative actions. The stations of Christ's life are segmented into a series of performative tableaux. I have elsewhere made claims for the reevaluation of the film as a feminist tract ("Performativity"), but reconsidering the text within a study of race has forced me to consider its racist aspects.

Blaché's version of the life of Christ employs a slightly feminist, though dominantly white and racist perspective toward the subject, and performativity in this film blends spectacle and realism in an unprecedented manner. I also view this film within a theoretical and historical perspective that highlights Alice Guy Blaché and her role in the development of a hybrid cinema that questions notions of "realism" and "artifice" in gendered performativity. Like many other filmmakers of the silent era, Blaché readily mixes staged studio settings with natural location shooting, a practice that continues today. However, the extreme stylization of her vision in *La Vie du Christ* effectively creates an alternative universe in which the protagonists of the film seem enshrined by each of the carefully framed compositions. Indeed, Blaché's film is almost a moving painting, in which the prescient naturalism of the performers seems at times strikingly removed from the constructed settings that dominate most of the production.

In *La Vie du Christ* white women are foregrounded as central characters and witnesses to the spectacle of Christ's birth. Christ himself is feminized, white, and eroticized. In general, performances in this film are unlike many of those of other films of the same period. Characters are suffused with familiarity, carnality, and corporeality. Sets combine highly artificial indoor *tableaux vivantes* with exterior scenes of natural lighting and neorealist staging. This hybrid construction of on-screen space is compounded by an odd mix of performative acting styles. Scenes of white family life are intercut with scenes of pageantry, yet the naturalistic acting in *La Vie du Christ* is mixed with overly theatrical performativity and artifice. In this departure from the film-acting styles of the period, Blaché refigures the performance of gender in the Christ parable, emphasizing and privileging women and children as active participants who perform in a hybrid spectacle that combines theatricality with an almost neorealist look.

Performances of hybridity in art and film have been, until recently, routinely criticized and dismissed out of hand. Artists and filmmakers whose work steps out of the boundaries of critical schools and aesthetic codes often find themselves categorically removed from the center of discursive fields of inquiry. One example of such an artist is Jacques-Joseph Tissot, a nineteenth-century painter who is celebrated for his Victorian renderings of elegant women but who is casually derided for his extensive, highly successful, and influential Bible illustrations. These illustrations, published in the highly popular and influential Tissot Bible, were the inspiration behind Blaché's lengthy filmic portrayal of the life of Christ. Tissot's Bible and Blaché's *Vie du Christ* share a preoccupation with performing the life of Christ in a hybrid style that combines realism, spiritualism, and literalism that perhaps seems crude, violent, or graphic compared to other films of the period. The flogging of Christ by the African centurions, for example, is presented in a near-documentary manner, despite the conscious artificiality of the settings and costumes. It is unusual in that even though one of the good three kings is black, all other black figures are marked as evil. For example, as noted earlier, blacks beat Jesus during the scourging, and two black figures hold the cross that Jesus is to be nailed to. It is striking that, in this version of the life of Christ, blacks are negative figures. White men are not prominently featured in the film, yet white women and children are "good" and helpful to Christ. In addition to its negative portrayal of blacks, *La Vie du Christ* is distinctly homophobic. Pontius Pilate is clearly an effeminate, flamboyant, gay-coded figure of evil.

The staged *tableau vivant* scenes in *La Vie du Christ* are performative in the manner described by Judith Butler. They are "performative in the sense that the essence or identity that they otherwise purport to express are fabrications manufactured and sustained through corporeal signs" (136). The corporeal signs of Jesus as a living being are stressed by the use of scores of white children, obviously nonactors, who pervade the entire spectacle. The baby Jesus is just that, a white baby brought onto the set and surrounded by onlookers. Jesus and Mary are distinctively unkempt, human; they reek of sensuality and corporeality. White women and children predominate in the composition. The viewer is startled by the degree to which Blaché portrays the spectacle of the birth and life of Christ as a family affair, with white children present at all times. The white figures are fully clothed and wear an approximation of a Roman toga: draped sheets, belted at the waist. The Africans are often half dressed, their chests prominently displayed. Clearly, blackness is associated with otherness. As Richard Dyer argues, "A naked body is a vulnerable body . . . clothes are bearers of prestige: to be without them is to lose prestige" (*White* 140).

The performative value of *La Vie du Christ* is important not only because of its ability to corporealize Jesus Christ but also because it is one of the few times that the cinematically rendered life of Christ has been infused with images of women and children as spectators, actors, and/or performers within the spectacle itself. The great number of white women and children further encourages audience identification with the film and opens up the finished production to a wider viewing audience. Blaché's representations of blackness are perhaps stereotypical of the Victorian era, yet her white women and white children are more modern; they look at the camera, directly address the viewer, and engage in interactions among themselves that are entirely incidental to the film's central narrative. In addition, her performers range across a wide variety of ethnic backgrounds, which constitutes a further departure from Victorian pictorial signification.

To the late-twentieth-century feminist, Blaché's feminism may seem to be a hybrid form of early white, middle-class feminism. The film is populated by white female angels, much in keeping with proscribed notions of Victorian femininity, yet these angels carry along the plot; they are not purely window dressing. Despite its racism, *La Vie du Christ* may be viewed as somewhat transgressive in its depiction of female whiteness. Alice Guy Blaché's performing women move away from overdeterminism, though they are certainly not devoid of subjectivity. The subjectivity of white women and children is rendered in a striking design of female performative enunciation. Indeed, this life of Christ is told through the eyes of the girl angels who guide us through the story. Each tableau begins with three white, powdered girls dressed as angels, holding up a title card. This is a life of Christ told from the point of view not only of angels holding title cards but of the white females *performing* and *enacting* the entire narrative. In the scene titled "Le Sommeil de Jésus" ("The Infant Jesus' Sleep"), there is only one white male adult to be found. The baby Jesus is surrounded by whites: eight girl angels and

60

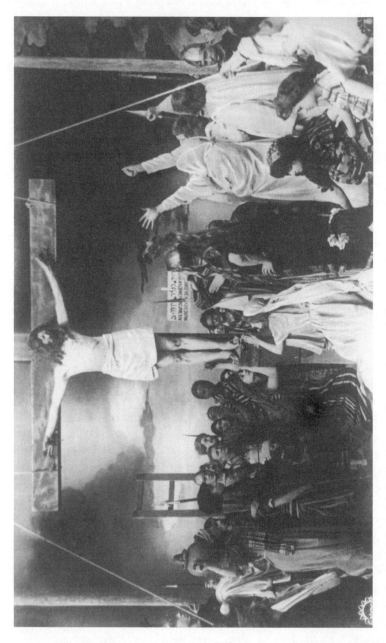

FIGURE 8. Black figures in attendance at the crucifixion of Christ in Alice Guy Blaché's film *La Vie du Christ* (1906). Courtesy Jerry Ohlinger Archives.

one woman figure (presumably Mary). The roles of adult white males in the life of Christ are downplayed.

The little white girls are hybridizations of the angel of the house of the nineteenth century. They are not passive, fainting, ethereal presences but instead diligently hardworking musicians in an unusual rendering of the life of Jesus. The angels look directly at the audience, as if to invite the viewer into the manufactured spectacle of realism, in a display of the redemptive possibilities of hybrid performance and decorative film space. Blaché values the supernatural girl angels as much as she does the other numerous "real" women and children in the film. Indeed, the sheer number of white women in the twenty-five scenes of *La Vie du Christ* seems designed to convey the feminization of the narrative of the life of Christ. Similarly, Christ's crucifixion is attended by scores of women and children. When Christ rises from the dead, the spectacle of the resurrection is seemingly facilitated by several young girls, who seem to *will* the event through the power of their white female gaze.

Indeed, Alice Guy Blaché was so successful in her melding of the real and the fantastic in *La Vie du Christ* that the film was later credited to other directors, such as Victorin Jasset, who was in actuality the assistant director of the film. Blaché straddled the world of the Victorian angel of the house and the newly emerging "New Woman," and she seems to have been able to draw, in life, from these seemingly incongruent models of feminine comportment. Like many other white women of her time, Blaché embodied both the values of the New Woman and of the angel of the house, but she remained firmly in the proscribed rules of white middle-class patriarchy. When she introduced blacks in her narratives, they were generally there to perform as threatening others or used as markers to highlight the goodness of whiteness or comic foils. In Blaché's *Matrimony's Speed Limit* (1913), for example, a young man must marry immediately to inherit a fortune. In desperation, he begins accosting women in the street for a suitable "instant mate," but he draws the line at a black woman he momentarily mistakes for white because of her veil. Her blackness suddenly apparent, the man runs away in horror, much to the young African American woman's surprise and consternation.

Though Blaché's film offers a useful counterpoint to such patriarchally dominated narratives as Cecil B. DeMille's *Ten Commandments* (1956) and Nicholas Ray's *King of Kings* (1961), her narrative inscribes performing whiteness into the story of Christ, yet she does so at the expense of blacks and blackness, even while she introduces an unprecedented, if highly problematic, feminist version of the life of Christ. Clearly, then, *La Vie du Christ* shows that Frankenberg's comments about feminism in the late twentieth century certainly apply to a text from the early twentieth century: "There were, it appeared, multiple ways in which the racism of the wider culture was simply being replayed in feminist locations" (*White Women* 3). Evading white complicity, especially in our feminist rereadings of lost or neglected texts, is tantamount to maintaining and upholding the norm of whiteness. One cannot "do feminism" without taking race, class, and other identity markers into consideration. This makes it highly problematic to work on women writers or filmmakers who championed feminism at the expense of others in racist, homophobic, classist texts. Nevertheless, I think it is important that we write about and examine such texts, openly dissecting their racism, homophobic, and classist attitudes.

Though most, if not all, of Alice Guy Blaché's films featured white protagonists and white narratives, a few of her films did prominently feature black lead characters. A recently rediscovered Blaché film, *A Fool and His Money* (1912), appears to have been aimed largely at black audiences and featured an all-black cast. Though the film is currently being recovered, many stills from the film are available (see McMahan, *Fool*). Briefly, *A Fool and His Money* is a comedy about what happens when a working-class black man suddenly comes into a windfall of money. Perhaps the alternative title, *Darktown Aristocrats,* best captures the fact that the humor derives from placing black actors in bourgeois settings and clothing. The jokes are around the issue of sudden prosperity. We see Sam (James Russell), the main character, recklessly spending his money on clothes, such as a top hat and tails, as well as an automobile with a chauffeur. He becomes engaged to a light-skinned black woman, Lindy, and at a reception is bamboozled in a card game. The "slick Mr. Tighe" and his friends cheat Sam out of his money. In one scene a barefooted black man is passed a card under the table with his foot. When Lindy learns that Sam has been swindled, she transfers her affections to Mr. Tighe, the man who "won" all of Sam's money. As Alison McMahan argues in an excerpt from her forthcoming book on Alice Guy Blaché (see McMahon, *Fool,* where the excerpt is posted), the film is certainly racist, but it also reflects "the dream of assimilation" associated with both immigrants and the black middle class. McMahan compares Blaché with black filmmaker Oscar

Micheaux, saying that what they "had in common was their outsider status to mainstream cinema." For Blaché, "assimilation meant taking on the stereotypes of the adopted culture" (McMahan, *Fool*). Blaché may have presented strong women characters who certainly behaved like feminists, especially given the time period, but she was subject to white, middle-class, bourgeois limitations when it came to issues of class and race. Even though she herself was a French immigrant to the United States, as McMahan concludes, "the shared concerns of class and assimilation did not prevent Guy from replicating the racist stereotypes of both French and American culture" *(Fool).* Though it is difficult to establish a complete understanding of the treatment of race in *A Fool and His Money* without seeing the fully restored film, it is safe to assume that the film engages in such stereotypes. Alice Guy Blaché is to be credited as an accomplished director who is being rewritten into film history, but it is important to take into account her heterocentrism and racism. She is a valuable example of an early hybrid type of feminist who spanned the eras of the Victorian angel of the house and the New Woman. She captured images that reflect a time of great social change. Her treatments of the other in *Making an American Citizen, La Vie du Christ,* and *A Fool and His Money* are as important as her treatments of female figures. Looking at her films underscores the complexity of revisiting captured images of the past.

Capturing an other is the project of narrative films, just as much as ethnographic film (and image) making is in a way seen as an extension of the ethnographic practice of denial of subjectivity and the privileging of the gaze of the captor over the "primitive," "exotic," "sexual," "backward," and "romantic" "savage." The definition of the clean white body is itself maintained by the insistent prevalence of images of others. Critics are remapping the landscape of cinema history as the center of struggle over ownership of the body, reminding us that cinema has been mired in patriarchal discourse. Film imagery is rooted in both a presence and an absence of images of slavery, colonialist appropriation of Native American, African, and female bodies, and a whole range of signifiers of bound bodies and captive knowledge, holding desire and resistance hostage to its referents.

As others have observed, *whiteness* as a category is maintained by a constant supply of colonialist imagery. Homosexuality is similarly othered to maintain its binary category of heterosexuality. To contain classed bodies, a whole system exists that attempts to erase class as much as it reinterprets it and perpetuates it. The female body is tied to the tracks, bound and gagged, held captive, in order to maintain gendered conditions, to define masculinity and femininity. It seems as if we are trapped in a need for binaries to support our taxonomies of subjectivity and objectivity. The image-production system itself is maintained to simulate reality (as Jean Baudrillard and others remind us). The simulation of reality provides the binary to experienced reality. But is there a way out of this self-enforced hegemony?

Rape-revenge films, as one example of the construction of whiteness, share with other films the ability to construct forms of alterity within the world of the corporeal visual construct. Existing in an all-white jungle of monstrous fantasies, such films as *Halloween* (1978), *I Spit on Your Grave* (1978), and the now popular and increasingly numerous grisly, white serial rapist-serial killer films (such as *Kalifornia* [1993] and *Henry: Portrait of A Serial Killer* [1986]) focus the viewer's conscious or unconscious attention on the constructs of whiteness and white power. This phenomenon suggests a recent resurgence of the attempt to resexualize and reenergize whiteness.

As it becomes increasingly noticeable and problematic to code African American men as monstrous sex criminals, recent films mark white-trash males as the embodiment of the other. Narratives of captivity and threat are increasingly white-on-white. This shift may begin to unravel a Gordian knot of related theoretical questions: What is behind the current proliferation of serial-killer films? Why do predominantly white audiences find the reinscription of white supremacy in the performative tropes of the serial murderer so attractive? Are whites attempting to sexualize and re-mark whiteness at the expense of those whites and blacks and others who are increasingly economically disenfranchised? How else does one account for the cultish appeal of Quentin Tarantino, whose *Pulp Fiction* (1994) single-handedly resuscitates white supremacy, homophobia, and misogyny as marketable concepts for a new, "hip" audience?

These cinematic texts include the birth of whiteness, the cult of gender, the definitions of class and ethnicity, the narratives of allowable sexual representation, and the renarration of the experience of African Americanness in American history. This immobilization is coupled with its own set of movement and resistances, but it still seems extraordinary to fathom the homogeneity, or at least the simulacrum or appearance of homogeneity, of Hollywood product in its sameness. The Baudrillardian powers of seduction of film narrative are powerful enough seemingly to "naturalize" orders and regimes, narratives and lore; it has taken film critics decades finally to credit audiences as coproducers of images instead of mere subjectified physical presences. Audiences share responsibility for the images produced by the Hollywood cinema factory and for the synthetic shaping of race and culture that has helped to define the American landscape of desire.

Though D. W. Griffith is often seen as the cinematographic father of racism (and of gendered white supremacy) in American cinema, we should remember that it was audiences and critics who made his films popular. Just as Adolf Hitler could not have implemented his plans for racial annihilation without a significant number of "willing executioners," neither could Griffith have popularized his outrageously racist and sexist ideologies without dependence on a culture willing to accept (and to coproduce) such images and narratives. The violence and repugnance of the narratives of the pro-KKK *Birth of a Nation* and *Broken Blossoms* (1919) were not aberrations, as one might be misled into thinking in looking through film history. Daniel Bernardi offers a remarkable discussion of Griffith's cinematic vision in his study of the filmmaker's early works, which were deeply involved in the on-screen construction of whiteness, race, ethnicity, and gender. Such Griffith films as *The Chink at Golden Gulch* (1910), *The Call of the Wild* (1908), *The Zulu's Heart* (1908), and *The Girls and Daddy* (1909) uphold the racist ideology of images in the much earlier films *Watermelon Patch* (Edwin S. Porter, 1905) and *A Nigger in the Woodpile* (Biograph, 1904), which construct "whiteness" in opposition to "blackness," with all that is white being artificially and synthetically elevated, and blackness aligned with a series of negative and/or childlike characteristics, thus inculcating the racist mechanism of the KKK as both a "paternal" order and an agency of social and cultural enforcement. The cultural "work" of articulating white dominance depended on inclusions and exclusions, narrations and denarrations, but this project was not possible without public approval and cooperation. Too many critics, I think, attempt to separate Griffith's stature as a great pioneering stylist from his racism. We should not set up Griffith's legacy as a binary, a binary that suggests that his development of parallel edging and narrative storytelling have (in such films as *The Lonedale*

Operator [1911]) nothing to do with his abilities to script white as the norm and nonwhite as outside the norm. Whiteness and whiteface—as coproduced by Griffith, other directors, such as Blaché, and audiences—are present both on-screen and off, but it is always dependent on blackness and nonwhiteness for its mirroring and othering process.

Writing about whiteness is so difficult because of its invisibility and its location as the norm. The invisibility of whiteness "secures white power by making it hard, especially for white people and their media[,] to 'see' whiteness" (Dyer, "White" 46); however, as Matthew Wray and Annalee Newitz note, it is equally important to remember that white supremacy is "the 'phallus' of the white race. It is an ideal which cannot even be achieved in a total sense" (146). Elusive and unachievable, it is, of course, in its own definition highly eroticized and fetishized.

To inculcate whiteness, such directors as Blaché and Griffith called upon the fallacious concept of the supposed "moral uplift of the races." It is revealing to chronicle the seriality with which Griffith approaches the same subjects—the sanctity of motherhood, the "virgin" woman confronted with threats of violence, the supposed benevolence of the patriarchy, the "legitimacy" of racism to uphold Victorian social values, just as the slave owners called upon religious sanctimoniousness in oppressing and martyring the "good slave," in the name of God. Critics working on race, ethnicity, and the issues around the constructedness of whiteness also continue to mark new ways of looking at looking. Some of the most exciting and perhaps disturbing theories in this area involve the mutability of the subject, and the introduction of malleable models of identity.

CHAPTER FOUR

THE BAD-WHITE BODY

In this chapter I seek to scrutinize white bodies in a series of films that foreground white self-hatred, fear, and whiteness. Eric Lott's "Whiteness of Film Noir" provides a useful template for this project. In his study of noir Lott found that

> Film noir is replete with characters of color who populate and signify the shadows of white American life in the 1940s. Noir may have pioneered Hollywood's merciless exposure of white pathology[,] but by relying on race to convey that pathology, it in effect erected a cordon sanitaire around the circle of corruption it sought to penetrate. Film noir rescues with racial idioms the whites whose moral and social boundaries seem in doubt. "Black film" is the refuge of whiteness. (83)

But while film noir is perhaps the last bastion of ungoverned whiteness, I find myself drawn to films that work in an oppositional manner toward whiteness, even if they sometimes inevitably foster a sense of closure and agency for white badness. These films don't really belong to a genre, and they often exclude any nonwhite characters. Science-fiction and horror films frequently feature unstable white bodies: white bodies out of control, invisible bodies, bodies missing hands, brains without skulls, monstrous eyeballs, bodies contaminated by nuclear fallout, bodies at war with their own corporeal existence. Such films as *The Hand* (1960), *The Head* (1959), *The Man without a Body* (1957), *The Brain That Wouldn't Die* (1962), *Attack of the 50 Foot Woman* (1958), *The Amazing Colossal Man* (1957), *The Incredible 2-Headed Transplant* (1971), and *The Incredible Shrinking Man* (1957) not only problematize whiteness but display the instability of white embodiedness and subjectivity and suggest a post-modern reworking of self with regards to whiteness. Considered to be trivial junk, camp, or trash cinema, these films have a devoted cult following among aficionados of bizarre cinema. They also have much to teach us about our attitudes toward the body and the ways in which it is colonized, gendered, raced, classed, and socialized.

In these films of the bad-white body, whiteness is usually associated with badness, war against the self, destruction, murder, death, and hypersexuality. Exploitation films are seen as tasteless, perhaps because they often straight white culture in a harsh light. Bodies out of control, they are white others to whiteness itself. They "perform" whiteness in the sense that Patricia J. Williams uses the phrase (10). In one of her "Diary of a Mad Law Professor" columns, Williams notes that racial identity was legally tied to "conduct and character," as well as to such better-known features as ancestry, voting rights, and "reputation and acceptance among others, both white and black" (10). The way to pass as white for someone defined as "black" had as much to do with behavior and a perception of "acting white" (for example, well mannered) as it did other factors.

> In courts throughout the South, the borderline statuses of the "enslaved white" and the "passing black" were methodically examined, defined and reduced to stereotypes that endure to this day. Putatively enslaved whites came mostly from the ranks of "poor whites," whom the common law generally disparaged as those with coarse features and bad manners; in contrast, "passing" blacks were those with "fine" features and deceptively good manners. (P. Williams 10)

As Thomas Cripps and others have noted, blackness in cinema is often associated with bad conduct, hypersexuality, monstrous behavior, and the threat of otherness. But what if the monster-other is not only white but in struggle with his own body, a self-reflective Janus face interminably attempting to destroy itself? I find it curious that such fascinating exemplars of white-on-white terror have been relegated to the dustbin of culture, trash films for laughs, enjoyed only at the level of camp, when they should be seriously considered for their problematizing of race, gender, sexuality, and ethnicity, but especially whiteness. They are cultural relics, examples of "bad" whites often at war with their own (sometimes) "good" selves. Even if they are exploitation films, they have cultural significance, especially since they appear in the 1950s through the late 1970s, a period of cultural change, most notably integration, decolonization, and the beginnings of civil rights.

> Exploitation [films] provide an important aesthetic and political prism through which the entire domain of cinematic theory can be rethought in the context of taste. In negotiating this increasingly urgent manoeuvre, film theory may confront itself precisely where it has convinced itself it should not exist: establishing conceptual alliances no longer reducible to the stultifying laws of taste. (Watson 82)

I am also in agreement with Joan Hawkins, who writes in *Cutting Edge* that "film representations can be *both* subversive and hegemonically contained" (215). One thing that I find fascinating about bad-white-body films is that they often suggest a postmodern definition of self, as defined here by Linda Hutcheon: "The postmodern way of defining the self (an internalized challenge to the humanist notion of integrity and seamless wholeness) has much to do with this mutual influencing of textuality and subjectivity" (83). Bad-white-body films challenge the integrity of the body and the wholeness of identity as much as they challenge the integrity and wholeness of whiteness. They also are generated from a space that problematizes and fragments the binaries *good* and *bad, moral* and *immoral,* as well as the notion of a *unified performing self.*

Take, for example, the spectacle of tragedy afforded the viewer in *The Amazing Colossal Man* (1957) and its sequel, *War of the Colossal Beast* (1958). The disease of the central character, Lieutenant Colonel Glenn Manning (played by Glenn Langan in the first film and look-alike Duncan "Dean" Parkin in the sequel) is brought on by exposure to a plutonium bomb explosion. Manning grows taller than fifty feet, the height attained by the main character of *Attack of the 50 Foot Woman;* perhaps his disease is, after all, the burden of whiteness itself and, in particular, "responsible" white maleness. Manning's body is burned by radiation (white man's science), and begins to grow completely "out of control," yet for all his size he spends much of the film (until his mind fails him and he is forced to resort to inarticulate grunts in a futile attempt to communicate with the outside world) bemoaning the fact that he is now "less than a man," especially when he's with his sympathetic if bewildered wife, Carol Forrest (Cathy Downs), with whom he can no longer associate as a human, much less as a sex partner. (In the sequel the Carol

70

FIGURE 9. Lieutenant Colonel Glenn Manning (Glenn Langan) in the home that no longer fits his unruly body in *The Amazing Colossal Man* (1957). Courtesy Jerry Ohlinger Archives.

Forrest character disappears and is replaced by Joyce Manning [Sally Fraser], Colonel Manning's sister, his wife having apparently deserted him.) I would argue that the source of Colonel Manning's pain is white hegemonic power, especially as it is associated with the military, who sanctioned the atomic tests that led to Manning's exposure to radiation. But perhaps the *Colossal* films also deploy Richard Dyer's ideas about the association of whiteness with death.

> The idea of whites as both themselves dead and as bringers of death is commonly hinted at in horror literature and film. . . . It is a cultural space that makes bearable for whites the exploration of the association of whiteness with death. . . . [T]his is the apotheosis of whiteness: to be destroyed by your own kind. (*White* 210–11)

It is as if the space of the colossal beast is a zone for the consideration of the power of hegemonic white America in the 1950s, and it is here, in tragic proportions, that whites were able to begin to look at the paradoxes of white power and its association with the death and destruction of its own people.

These paradoxes show up clearly in the 1958 sequel, *War of the Colossal Beast.* In the first film Colonel Manning (Glenn Langan) goes over Boulder Dam and is declared dead (this brief sequence was shot in color; the rest of the film is in black-and-white). But in the sequel Manning (now Dean Parkin) is alive and hiding in the Mexican countryside. Lonely, horribly disfigured, his mind gone, the giant Manning survives by overturning rural grocery trucks and scavenging through the wreckage for food. The viewer sympathizes with him as a grotesque white other. White society, even the military, his ostensible home, has no idea what to do with him, just as white society was ill-prepared to manage and aid returning veterans from World War II and Korea. The "authorities" tranquilize Manning and shackle him in chains inside a hangar at Los Angeles International Airport, but he escapes and terrorizes Los Angeles. The sequel contains a number of flashbacks to the first film (no doubt for budgetary considerations, as these are some of the more spectacular scenes of destruction), but they serve to remind the viewer that Manning's ordeal is unending, cutting him off from society completely. At the end of the film, Manning intentionally walks into a set of high-tension power lines. He cannot communicate with the outside world; he can only communicate (through memories) with himself. Yet the paradoxes remain unresolved even as Manning commits suicide, and the film leaves itself open to a number of conflicting interpretations.

Paradoxes are part of the postmodern condition. "While unresolved paradoxes may be unsatisfying to those in need of absolute and final answers, to postmodernism thinkers and artists they have been the source of intellectual energy that has provoked new articulations of the postmodern condition" (Hutcheon 21). *War of the Colossal Beast* refers to the war that one bad white-other wages against society as much as it refers to society's discomfort with returning war veterans. It is interesting to note that the authorities only give up on Colonel Manning when they think his mind has "gone." When he loses his faculties and powers of speech, he seemingly loses whiteness and becomes a liminal white other. He gives up his white identity, even his human identity. Now Manning is seen only as a monster who must be destroyed. Even his own sister encourages him to kill himself, ostensibly to save a busload of children he holds aloft near the Griffith Park Planetarium. Though the film seemingly allows for closure, it also problematizes whiteness and white male conduct, specifically blind allegiance to the armed forces. Like postmodern performance studies alluded to by Jon McKenzie, the *Colossal* films work in the space of the liminal and "theorize performative genres as liminal, that is, as 'in-between' times/spaces in which social norms are broken apart, turned upside down, and played with" (220).

Problematic liminal whiteness is a hallmark of the bad-white-body film. This trash film investigates cultural amnesia, the forgetting of the price of war. That price is maleness itself. No wonder Colonel Manning keeps repeating that he feels like "less than a man." He is treated as an other to whiteness and to white maleness. He is out of control, yet the authorities do not fault themselves for the nuclear accident, nor do they credit Colonel Manning for his war efforts. Viewing the film from a postmodern perspective, it is clear that this film is in many ways radically subversive for a film of the 1950s. It reminds us that, as Hutcheon suggests, "The act of problematizing is, in a way, an act of restoring relevance to something ignored or taken for granted. . . . What postmodernism does is not only to remind us of this, but also to investigate our amnesia" (229). The space of enunciation, the performance of whiteness in the *Colossal* films underscores the unstable configuration of whiteness at odds with itself.

It is telling that these films appear in the 1950s, when social codes were both regressing, in terms of attitudes toward women and minorities, and also advancing with the beginnings of the women's liberation and civil rights efforts. The cheap sci-fi exploitation vehicle allowed for a space in which the social conduct of white society is highly criticized. Culture—especially white male culture—is scrutinized and constructed as untenable, which demonstrates that the cultural performance of whiteness is subject to instability. In the words of Homi K. Bhabha,

> It is only when we understand that all cultural statements and systems are constructed in this contradictory and ambivalent space of enunciation, that we begin to understand why hierarchical claims to the inherent originality or "purity" of cultures are untenable, even before we resort to empirical historical instances that demonstrate their hybridity. (37)

In this sense the films of the bad-white body constitute an expression of the dichotomy inherent in the artificially constructed performance of whiteness.

Grotesque proportions are an important feature in bad-white-body films, just as shrunken bodies and out-of-control body parts are integral. Performances of bad-white bodies, grotesque and liminal, disruptive of whiteness, are certainly not rare in American cinema. These repeated performances become an "antinorm" of sorts, a norm of othered whiteness. As McKenzie states in a study of performativity, it is "through repeated performances [that] these norms become sedimented *as* (and not in) gendered bodies" (221). I want to bring up the specter of gender as I move to another film, this one featuring a huge, monstrous, white female body, the infamous *Attack of the 50 Foot Woman* (1958). In the film Nancy Fowler Archer (Allison Hayes), an alcoholic millionaire unhappily married to worthless fortune-hunter Harry Archer (William Hudson), grows to gargantuan proportions after she is raped by a thirty-foot-tall, semi-transparent, balding alien (Michael Ross, who also plays Tony, the owner of a sleazy bar and hotel, where much of the film's action takes place) during a nighttime drive in the desert. Just as in the *Colossal* films, the white authorities are stumped by the appearance of an out-of-control white body, in this case a female body, a rape victim, and an angry woman who finds that her husband is cheating on her with a "lower-class" white woman, Honey Parker (Yvette Vickers). Just as we saw Colonel Manning chained by the white authorities, we now see Nancy Archer similarly chained up in her mansion by two befuddled white doctors, who give her massive injections of morphine with an elephant syringe in a futile

FIGURE 10. Nancy Archer (Allison Hayes) is about to be raped by a thirty-foot giant in *Attack of the 50 Foot Woman* (1958). Courtesy Jerry Ohlinger Archives.

attempt to keep her under control. In the meantime, her husband, "Handsome Harry," spends all of his time and Nancy's money in Tony's bar, where he is either bedding down Honey Parker in the rooms upstairs or plotting ways to push his wife over the brink of sanity, so that he can inherit the Star of India Diamond, along with the rest of her millions. In the film's justifiably brutal conclusion, Nancy Archer finally breaks free of the mansion that has become her prison and stalks into town, where Harry is drinking himself into oblivion at Tony's. Without hesitation, the fifty-foot Nancy rips the roof off the building, grabs Harry with one enormous hand, kills Honey by dropping huge chunks of debris on her, and then commits suicide and murder by walking into a conveniently located set of high-tension power lines (as in *War of the Colossal Beast*) with the squashed Harry still in her hand, killing them both.

To understand the numerous bad-white bodies in *Attack of the 50 Foot Woman,* it is important to consider white performance of both class and gender. The *Colossal* films were very much about angry, unfairly treated, white male veterans. *Attack of the 50 Foot Woman* is about a bored, alcoholic, stay-at-home wife and is thus a critique of gender roles of the 1950s. The film clinically examines 1950s marriage and gender roles, using the schlocky atmosphere of the exploitation vehicle to bring up such issues as rape, class difference, and the breakdown of white heterosexual coupling. As is often the case, it is the exploitation film that offers the opportunity to talk about and perform subjects and social issues that are considered taboo in mainstream culture. Indeed, a white woman is subject here to rape, a cheating husband, and medical mistreatment at the hands of white culture, a culture that is ultimately responsible for her death. Few films of the 1950s dealt with rape, with the exception of director Ida Lupino's *Outrage* (1950), which begins with a harrowing white-on-white rape at a young woman's workplace by a fellow employee (never named in the film, but played by Albert Mellen). The victim of the assault, Ann Walton (Mala Powers), is more psychically damaged by the disinterest of white society in her plight than she is physically damaged by the attack itself. Society, particularly in America in the 1950s, always blames the victim. Indeed, I would argue that *Outrage* is much more critical of white society's inability to deal with the rape of women than the act of rape itself. Lupino deftly handles the issues that surrounded rape in the postwar era and that still, to a large degree, persist today; women are assumed to have somehow been guilty of "leading on" their own rapists.

Nathan Hertz (as Nathan Juran), who directed *Attack of the 50 Foot Woman,* and his scenarist, Mark Hanna, are also guilty of blaming the victim in this film. Both the police and her attending physicians suggest that Nancy's gigantism as a consequence of the rape (which no one believes happened) is somehow her fault, and she must be silenced for suggesting that white men rape and abuse their own white women. The film is, of course, rife with mixed messages undermining the supposed stability of white heterocentrism and the institution of marriage. If the film and its characters blame Nancy Archer for her condition, the audience, at least, wants to see her exact vengeance. Nancy, like the colossal beast, becomes a sort of white version of the "noble savage." By the film's conclusion the audience is completely sympathetic as Nancy destroys both herself and the cheating pair, Harry and Honey, themselves embodiments of the sexually out of control bad-white body.

Much is made of class in the film. Nancy Archer is coded as upper class by her jewelry, her mansion, her butler, and her cultured behavior. Her deportment is in sharp contrast to that of her husband, Harry, and the slatternly Honey Parker, who are definitively classed by their behavior, clothing, and performances. The rule of thumb for the lower working classes in white culture is that they are "not supposed to be seen," according to Peter Hitchcock (21), but Harry and Honey are constantly on display, flaunting their relationship throughout the town, despite the gravity of Nancy's condition. In an article about the problems inherent in portrayals of working-class whites, Hitchcock writes: "'You're not supposed to be seen,' but the paradox of working-class subjectivity is that you must be seen in order to confirm that class is there and negotiable in stable and unthreatening ways. . . . The 'must be seen' of working-class subjectivity is intimately connected to modes of representation and power" (21).

On-screen African Americans in the past shared this conundrum with working-class white others: you are not supposed to exist, but when you do, you are to represent otherness to whiteness, specifically classed whiteness. One would certainly not find such unsavory low-class figures as Handsome Harry or Honey Parker in mainstream 1950s television series, such as *The Donna Reed Show* or *Father Knows Best.* More likely such figures would turn up as lowlifes on *Dragnet* or *Racket Squad.* Harry is a consummate drunk and womanizer; he cares little for his wife and openly carries on his affair with Honey. Their scenes in Tony's honky-tonk are excellent signifiers of the downside of the 1950s American dream. Moreover, not only do Harry and Honey choose to live in squalor, they also treat even each other badly. Honey suggestively hangs on Harry's shoulders or hips in every scene of the film the two share; when they dance, it is always a slow, drunken bump and grind. Their conversation is limited to ordering more drinks, sex, how to swindle Nancy out of her money and/or kill her, all the better to get out of town and "live a little." Discouraged from working outside the home, Nancy becomes a 1950s housewife. But she becomes an alcoholic instead of fulfilling the role of the proper heteronormative mate.

There is a notable silence about class in much film theory, but I think it is class intersecting with gender that makes *Attack of the 50 Foot Woman* such an important example of the bad-white-body film. An interesting correlative is the Korl Woman in Rebecca Harding Davis's "Life in the Iron Mills." Here we have another gigantic woman associated with working-class life. Eric Schocket, who investigates this figure, associates her with "signifiers of blackness."

> Even the Korl Woman, a statue that figures the terrible hunger of working-class life, turns out to be "a woman, white of giant proportions," carved from industrial material with an eerie "flesh-tint." Rising out of the soot and blackness and gesturing with outstretched white arms toward the sky, she is nothing so much as a racial figure for working-class possibility. And standing as she does in the center of what we have come to consider the germinal text of American industrial fiction, she casts a long white shadow that we have yet to see fully.
>
> For in what we might call the irony of white servitude, Davis employs linguistic conventions that invite readers to discover a new race but gives them instead a new class (the working class) whose white bodies are inscribed with uncanny signifiers of blackness. (47)

Are bad-white bodies, especially lower-class bad-white bodies, raced? Or is this notion too simplistic? White consciousness is related to terror. It is deployed through oppressive white looks, looks that privilege and looks that oppress. I am drawn to the idea that lower- or working-class whites can be inscribed with signifiers of blackness, but I stubbornly maintain that these signifiers have more to do with an attempt to configure whiteness as a construction that is falsely stable. It should come as no surprise to us that lower- or middle-class whites are othered and perhaps even raced, as David Roediger, Annalee Newitz, Matt Wray, and others have asserted. I do not want to suggest that race is simply substituted for class. Whiteness is above all about sublimating forms of identity. Bad-white-body films allow a culturally agreed upon space for those sublimated tropes to be rehearsed and performed. Bad-white-body films expose myths and lies perpetuated by dominant culture. *Attack of the 50 Foot Woman* is not just a campy trash film fit for bad film festivals. It is, rather, a critique of whiteness, the nuclear family, and all the falsely utopian visions these constructs are associated with. Seen in this light, the film is a surreal riff on *Outrage*, presenting the white raped woman as an out-of-control gargantuan figure. The white authorities' inability to deal with a white raped female is an idea dealt with in serious dramatic fashion in *Outrage;* even so, when the film was released, many critics thought that the subject itself was in such poor taste that the film should never have been produced. In *Outrage* a compassionate psychiatrist helps Ann Walton rejoin society, in an ending that is simultaneously hetero-centric and imposed upon the film because of the censorship constraints of the Eisenhower era. But it is in the surreal schlockfest of *Attack of the 50 Foot Woman* that the white woman has revenge on society. She squeezes and electrocutes her husband to death for his cheating and complete lack of regard for her as an alcoholic rape victim. The problem, of course, is that she must die. The narrative demands it; the audience demands it; the Production Code demands it. The formulaic genre of the film demands it. White blood lust demands it. Nancy Archer is a sexual white female who has gone out of control, and, like Colonel Manning, she must be destroyed. The ads for the film describe her thusly: "See a female colossus . . . her mountainous torso, skyscraper limbs, giant desires" (qtd. in Weldon 26). It's obvious: Nancy Archer must die because she hasn't performed her white femininity correctly. "For a woman, performing whiteness meant acting out purity and moral virtue" (P. Williams 10). Harry, her husband, must also die because he has performed male whiteness inappropriately, and he has failed to adhere to a classed gentleman's code of conduct. Bad whiteness, for both, ultimately is out-of-control sexuality, something frequently associated with blackness and with lower-class performativity.

Rape is at the center of another important bad-white-body film, *The Beast Within* (1982). In this film Michael MacCleary (Paul Clemens) is a teenage boy who was conceived when his mother was raped by a swamp monster. At the age of seventeen, he begins to become an insect and sheds his human skin. *The Beast Within* is another bad-white film; it conflates low-class behavior (in this case within the bounds of Southern society) with rampant sexuality and animal depravity. The rape in *The Beast Within* seems associated with incest and/or the black male rapist myth; as the young man mutates, he literally sheds his whiteness and becomes an animal who decapitates, kills, and eats anyone who gets in his way. This brings up the specter of white women being raped by aliens, swamp monsters, giants—everything but actual white men. There are, of course, numerous films that feature white-on-white rape, which is, in fact, becoming a staple of the postmillennial cinematic consciousness, along with Hollywood's preoccupation with an endless plague of serial killers, each more violent than the last. But the white woman continues to be at the mercy of the other, suggesting that American white culture cannot end its fascination with the trope of the black male rapist who was so definitively ground into the white imagination in such films as *Birth of a Nation*. The fact is that white women are most frequently raped by white men, often members of their families, as a matter of pure statistics.

Perhaps deflecting white-on-white rape onto monsters is one way to deflect shame and blame. Bad-white-body films that feature nonhuman rapists suggest shame and guilt but in the safe space of the campy exploitation film. Rita Felski has done considerable analysis of shame and guilt in Western societies.

> Until recently, it was often claimed that Western societies were guilt cultures rather than shame cultures, and researchers focused most of their attention on the analysis of guilt. There is now an upsurge of interest in shame as a cultural and psychological phenomenon of continuing relevance. The distinction between shame and guilt can be schematically defined as follows. Guilt is a sense of inner badness caused by a transgression of moral values; shame by contrast is a sense of failure or lack in the eyes of others. It has less to do with infractions of morality than with interactions of social codes and a consequent fear of exposure, embarrassment, and humiliation. (39)

Many bad-white-body films are obviously steeped in white guilt and shame and are displaced in quasi-anticolonialist films. One fine example of this type of film is the British-made *Dr. Terror's House of Horrors* (1965). The film tells the story of five doomed men who share a railway compartment with a tarot reader, Dr. Sandor Schreck (Peter Cushing). One is killed by a female werewolf; another is trapped with his family in his house by an out-of-control vine with paranormal intelligence. A jazz musician is attacked when he copies and then performs in public secret Haitian music that he has been specifically told not to play. At the subtextual level, these are bad-white figures who get their due because they continue to act as colonialists in a world that was increasingly decolonizing itself, as many African countries started to declare their independence in the 1950s and 1960s. An art critic, Franklyn Marsh (Christopher Lee), ruins the career of artist Eric Landor (Michael Gough) with a string of negative reviews in the press and then, for good measure, runs Landor down with his car, severing Landor's hand. Landor's severed hand then seeks out Marsh and causes his car to swerve off the road, severely injuring the critic. As the ambulance drivers take Marsh away from the scene of the wreck, one of them comments, "He'll never see again . . . still, there are plenty of things a blind man *can* do," as Marsh screams in agony.

The murderous severed white hand, unswervingly focused on revenge, is prominently featured in a number of bad-white-body films. In *The Hands of Orlac* (1961) Stephen Orlac (Mel Ferrer), a concert pianist, is given a replacement pair of hands after he loses both of his own hands in an accident. Unfortunately for Stephen, the hands that are grafted onto his body once belonged to a murderer, and as a result Stephen finds himself compelled to commit a series of crimes. As events unfold, Orlac is blackmailed by the unsavory magician Nero (Christopher Lee), who surmises what has transpired. The discrepancy between the white body of an upper-class pianist and the hands of a lower-class killer places whiteness in conflict with itself within a body that cannot contain both kinds of whiteness. In another version of the same story, *Hands of a Stranger* (1962), pianist Vernon Paris (James Stapleton) has his mutilated hands replaced by a surgeon. Paris finds himself unable to play the piano as a result and seeks revenge on the doctor who performed the surgery. Both films suggest a conflation of guilt and shame, but shame—caused by class conflict that takes place in the bodies of white men—seems to be the dominant emotion. Dislocated from their own bodies, their own class, both figures exemplify Felski's definition of shame.

> Some social conditions are thus more likely than others to induce a sense of shame. . . . [T]hose who are poor often experience shame when their poverty is exposed before the eyes of others. Shame, in other words, rises out of a discrepancy between certain norms and values and others perceived as superior.

The opportunities for experiencing shame increase dramatically with geographic and social forms of mobility, which provide an infinite array of chances for failure, for betraying by word or gesture that one does not belong to one's environment. (39)

The 1960 film *The Hand* tells the story of two British soldiers who are captured in Burma during World War II. They refuse to give information to the enemy, and as a result their hands are amputated. Their captain is the lone traitor who cooperates with the enemy. Years later, London is plagued by a series of grisly murders in which all of the victims have their hands amputated. A variation on castration anxiety is certainly at work here, but psychoanalytic methodology is not the only effective approach to these films. I agree with Kobena Mercer, who encourages a postmodern approach in *Welcome to the Jungle,*

Instead of an authoritative position, in which criticism reaches for the definitive judgment of value, it may be helpful to conceive of it as an ongoing conversation or dialogue that seeks to deepen our knowledge of the way texts "work" as they circulate in the contingent and contradictory circumstances of the public sphere. In this approach, it is not even necessary to construct a general or definitive framework for interpretation, as what arises instead is a practice of interruption, which does not aim to have the last word on the aesthetic value of a given text, but which recognizes the contextual character of the relations between authors, texts and audiences as they encounter each other in the worldly spaces of the public sphere. (252)

I am interested in the manner in which these "amputee films" allow for a sort of white splitting of identity, a space where shame and guilt can be disrupted or identified, a space where white audiences could flexibly identify in an intersubjective state with good/bad, class/not classed, male/female whites. As I noted in *Captive Bodies,* jungle films, such as *She* (which has been filmed many times), *Tarzan, the Ape Man,* and *Trader Horn,* "exist primarily to construct whiteness" (63). Similarly, bad-white-body films exist to construct whiteness through raising the specter of otherness *within* the body of whites.

As Dyer writes in *Stars,* film stars "embody social values that are to some degree in crisis" (25) and "serve to mask people's awareness of themselves as class members by reconstituting social differences in the audience . . . to obscure the political issues they embody" (27). Peter Cushing embodies a significant example of such a star. Cushing made a career of horror movies for Hammer Films and its chief competitor, Amicus, British companies that specialized in fantasy and science-fiction films. A frequent player in bad-white-body films, Cushing sometimes performed the bad-white figure and sometimes the good-white figure. He plays *both* in *The Skull* (1965), as Dr. Christopher Maitland, a professor of metaphysics who buys the stolen skull of the Marquis de Sade from Marco (Patrick Wymark), an unscrupulous antiques dealer, and soon becomes its servant. The skull wills him to commit numerous murders, and the audience is invited to participate vicariously in Maitland's crimes through the use of a series of point-of-view shots through the eyes of the skull, which brings up the issue of the performativity of the *audience* in bad-white-body films. *The Skull* allows the audience both to participate in bad-white performativity and to witness its consequences. This device smacks deeply of white colonial arrogance and traditional Western discourse's reliance on a "darkness within whiteness" (that which is capable of murder, rape, decapitation, dismemberment, and other atrocities). The history of white colonial arrogance and conquest is primarily a tale of the conquest and control of space and peoples. In these bad-white-body films the terrain of conquest is the white *body*, over which whiteness attempts to display mastery. The all-white world inhabited by these films is infected with unspoken desires, sexual jealousies, murderous frenzies, inchoate insanity, and malign evil. Western ideology, dependent on dualism, reinforces the need to produce such performances of whiteness. In such films the bad-white body is usually conquered, but the films remind whites that dualism exists in the white body and its performances and cannot be summoned forth without consequences.

This dualism often comes in the form of vicious and blatant misogyny, as in the film *The Brain That Wouldn't Die* (1962). Dr. Bill Cortner (Jason Evers) is a brilliant white surgeon who accidentally decapitates fiancée Jan Compton (Virginia Leith) in a driving accident. Instead of letting Compton die, Cortner immediately takes her head back to his basement laboratory and keeps it alive in a developing tray, constantly replenished with blood. The desperate Jan wants only to die and eventually complains so incessantly that the surgeon puts tape over her mouth. Cortner has plans of his own; intent on finding a suitable body for his fiancée's head, Cortner begins frequenting a series of sleazy strip clubs, looking for a candidate for his grafting experiment. *The Brain That Wouldn't Die*

83

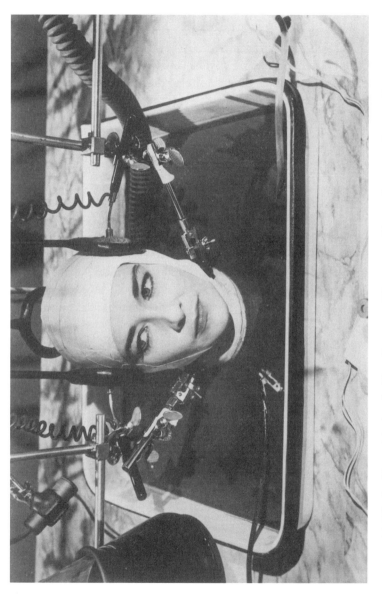

FIGURE 11. The bodiless white head of Jan Compton (Virginia Leith) in *The Brain That Wouldn't Die* (1962). Courtesy Jerry Ohlinger Archives.

paints the white scientist as wholly amoral and sexually obsessed, just as the scientists in the *Colossal* films, *The Skull,* and *The Hands of Orlac* are also morally bankrupt. Jan Compton, a now bodiless head, a single body part, is a white woman deprived of both agency and ability to alter her circumstances. However, as the film nears its appalling conclusion, Jan's head develops telepathic power, which enables her to control a half-human, half-beast monster, a "white thing" that Cortner keeps locked in a laboratory closet. The sum total of all his surgical failures to date, the white thing, which is possessed of superhuman strength, inevitably breaks out of its prison and is revealed to be a pastiche of arms, legs, eyes, and hands culled from previous surgical experiments. The creature sets the lab on fire, exacting Jan's vengeance, even as the flames consume her bandage-wrapped head. Another film that features a disembodied head is aptly titled *The Head* (1959; originally titled *Die Nackte und der Satan*), a West German film in which one Dr. Ood (Horst Frank) intentionally removes the head of his aging colleague, Professor Abel (Michel Simon), to keep his mind alive. "Your brain made you great! The rest doesn't count!" Ood shouts. But Abel is unimpressed and implores Ood to end the experiment. Predictably, however, Ood has other ideas and becomes obsessed with the idea of transplanting the head of his hunchbacked nurse, Irene (Karin Kernke), onto the body of a striptease dancer. Just as in *The Brain That Wouldn't Die,* Ood is soon off cruising the strip clubs, looking for the perfect subject for his experiment. Perhaps the most ghastly aspect of *The Head,* however, is not the misogyny of the plot but the fact that Abel is played by the great Michel Simon, who once starred in Jean Renoir's classic *Boudu Saved from Drowning* (1932). Fortunately, this was not the great actor's final film, although he kept up a busy schedule of low-budget films during his last years; perhaps one would rather remember Simon in his later years for his great performance in *The Two of Us* (1967), Claude Berri's film in which Simon's character, an aging anti-Semite who nevertheless shelters a young Jewish boy during World War II, represents another defective white man whose humanist values are restored by the devotion of a child.

The colonized medical gaze, a predominately white gaze, is associated with death in the bad-white-body film. Professor Steve March (John Agar) is a white nuclear physicist in *The Brain from Planet Arous* (1957) who finds himself under the telepathic influence of a floating brain from the planet Arous. A rival alien brain takes possession of March's dog, in the hope of thwarting the first brain's plans for world domination. At the end of the film, it is March's white girlfriend, Sally Fallon (Joyce Meadows), who attacks the "bad brain" with an ax, killing it. In *The Brain* (*Ein Toter sucht seinen Mörder* [1962]), yet another adaptation of Curt Siodmak's novel *Donovan's Brain* (which was filmed under that title in 1953 and under the title *The Lady and the Monster* in 1944), a doctor keeps alive the brain of a ruthless white businessman after a plane crash. As in the novel, the bad white brain gradually takes possession of the scientist's consciousness. *Donovan's Brain* (1953) stars Lew Ayres as Dr. Patrick Cory, whose mind is possessed by the will of the same ruthless business magnate whose white brain, this time, is deposited in a fish tank. In *Brain of Blood* (1972) Dr. Lloyd Trenton (Kent Taylor) is a malevolent brain-transplant specialist whose experiments ultimately result in dwarves and monsters. Chained white women abound in the ghastly, grim scientific lab of cinematic whiteness. The blatant misogyny of bad-white-body films is also evident in the 1981 version of *The Hand,* directed by Oliver Stone. When comic-book artist Jon Lansdale (Michael Caine) loses his drawing hand in a car wreck, his shrill, unsympathetic wife, Anne (Andrea Marcovicci), taunts him as a failure and takes a new lover. Unable to keep drawing the comic strip that had brought him to prominence, he is forced to earn a meager living teaching at a community college. One by one his female students start to disappear. Lansdale's hand, of course, is responsible, but Lansdale has no awareness of his severed hand's activities. As with the other films discussed here, the white man is shown as being ultimately not responsible for his own body's actions and his own inner desires. This duality allows a splitting of consciousness and conscience. In all these body-part films white badness is depicted as being not responsible for its actions. Thus Lansdale's misogyny is not a function of the whole man but of only part of his white body.

The Creeping Flesh (1973) manages to explore the fear of scientific experimentation even further. Peter Cushing plays Emmanuel Hildern, a colonial scientist of the Victorian era who returns to London from Papua New Guinea touting his new discovery: he can grow white flesh on a skeleton. His evil brother, James (Christopher Lee), steals the regenerating skeleton, which begins to dissolve without Emmanuel's attentions. The message is clear: white flesh cannot be duplicated or replicated. By the film's end Emmanuel has been committed to an asylum for the insane for his crimes. Whiteness, especially in British horror films of the 1960s and 1970s, is often equated with brutality and recklessly ill-advised science. Perhaps bubbling under these films is a hefty dose of colonialist guilt combined with a concomitant fear of medical science and its future. Further, I would suggest that bad-white-body films exist and multiply because of white shame and white fear of its own hybridity. Whiteness exists only when hybridity and otherness are erased; in a world of rampant hybridity, however, it is impossible to maintain hegemonic whiteness. Nowhere is that more true than at the site of the body and the soul, and no one is more at odds with and in touch with body and soul than the white scientist figure.

White science (read *bad whiteness*) has been responsible for the introduction of lethal nuclear radiation, and this bad-white science is at the center of *The Incredible Shrinking Man* (1957). While on a fishing boat in the first few minutes of the film, Scott Carey (Grant Williams) is exposed to a mysterious, potentially radioactive mist. Instead of growing to an enormous height like the man in the *Colossal* films, Carey begins, ever so gradually, to shrink. At first his clothes are loose, and he thinks he's lost a couple of pounds; soon he must wear children's clothing; finally, he must dress in an improvised loincloth cut from a handkerchief. Like the colossal man, the incredible shrinking white man watches helplessly as his marriage to Louise Carey (Randy Stuart) falls apart. He is terrorized by his own cat and is nearly devoured by a spider in the family's basement, where his diminutive size makes it impossible for his wife to locate or even hear him. The film's subtext certainly bespeaks castration anxiety, but I would argue that it also bespeaks fear of a diminishment of whiteness and the power that whiteness conveys. By 1957 black men had attained *some* degree of equality, in both the military and mainstream society. White maleness was in trouble, or at least white males felt that it was in trouble, but women—white women— were beginning to make real strides in the workplace. For all the effort to define the fifties as the *Leave It to Beaver* decade, the reality speaks otherwise. White men's power was decreasing in proportion to the rise of white women's power, especially as consumers. One could argue that the civil rights movement was beginning to mark a shift in white power, but more important in the reading of this film is the deep-seated fear of whiteness itself as an unattainable phantom figure. Scott Carey's personal narrative in *The Incredible Shrinking Man* begins with a happy white nuclear family. Carey's family and friends are initially supportive, even

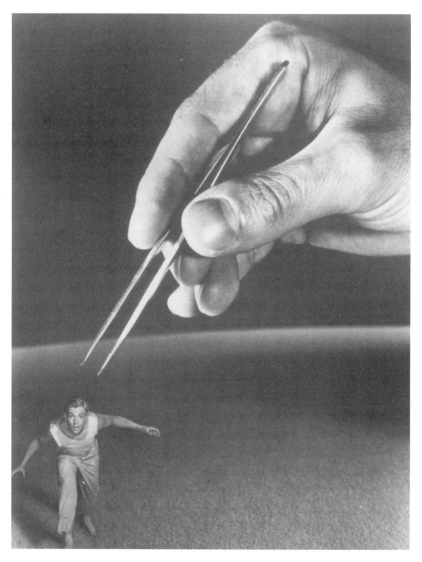

FIGURE 12. Scott Carey (Grant Williams) becomes a minute particle in the immense universe in *The Incredible Shrinking Man* (1957). Courtesy Jerry Ohlinger Archives.

after he begins to shrink. But they abandon Carey when they can no longer see him. White performativity in *The Incredible Shrinking Man* questions the historical validity of the dominance of white maleness in the 1950s. As Scott says in the film, "Easy enough to talk of soul and spirit and essential worth, but not when you're three feet tall." In a manner that is still striking today, the film encourages the audience to question the authenticity of "truth" of the primacy of the white nuclear family in a rather postmodern way. As Hutcheon asks of another text,

> Does the obvious performativity of the text really replace truth or does it, rather, question *whose* notion of truth gains power and authority over others and then examine the process of how it does so? . . . [I]t is also a very postmodern strategy, and here leads to the acknowledgment, not of truth, but of truths in the plural, truths that are socially, ideologically, and historically conditioned. (18)

The Incredible Shrinking Man is perhaps one of the more important bad-white-body films because it deals with white culture's lack of compassion for the fallen white hero. Scott Carey's house is no longer a haven; it is a series of deadly traps. As the film nears its conclusion, Carey continues to shrink with each passing hour, until he is small enough to squeeze through the screen mesh of a basement window and leaves the former safety of his split-level home. It is only outside this white nuclear family home that Carey experiences any sense of hope. Looking up at the stars, Carey decides he's going to continue his struggle as long as he can still see the heavens, and he delivers a fervent voice-over on the value of life, no matter how small it may be. As he shrinks smaller and smaller, the film ends with the possibility that Carey may be absorbed by the cosmos, becoming a part of the earth and the planets, leaving his human aspect behind entirely.

To this point, I've considered only all-white bad-white-body films. Many films, however, include bodies out of control that are problematized by being about hybrids of white and black bodies, including *The Cosmic Man* (1959) and *The Thing with Two Heads* (1972). These films remind us that race as an identity is constructed through an agreed-upon relationship:

> An *individual* is a relationship composed of the different identities which participants in the relationship retain. An individual is, inevitably, an asym-

metric relationship, since some-*body* will believe that their cluster of beliefs about an individual is about them-self, while other people will believe that the individual is some-*body* else. (Monk 31)

This idea of an agreed-upon relationship is put to the test in *The Cosmic Man,* another 1950s sci-fi thriller, starring John Carradine as the Cosmic Man, a friendly but misunderstood alien who has, at times, black skin and a white shadow. He can pass as white and, if need be, attain invisibility, but he passes, perhaps most interestingly, as *human* by wearing a hat, sunglasses, and trench coat. The film views him as a well-meaning alien with a bad body because he has to work at passing for a white human male. He means no harm to humans, and in fact he cures a quadriplegic child. At the end of the film, he must be destroyed to satisfy the requirements of the genre, but two sympathetic scientists, Dr. Karl Sorenson (Bruce Bennett) and Kathy Grant (Angela Greene), believe in the alien's mission. *The Cosmic Man* thus puts race itself on trial, under detailed visual scrutiny. The film forces the audience to question the validity of race as a "scientific" category. Not surprisingly, race leaves its strongest imprint on the human body in the supposedly authoritative field of science. K. Anthony Appiah and Amy Gutmann, whose work aggressively challenges the validity of biological race, argue,

Throughout the nineteenth century the term "race" came increasingly to be regarded, even in ordinary usage, as a scientific term. Like many scientific terms, its being in use among specialists did not stop its being used in everyday life. Treating it as a scientific term meant not that it was only for use by scientists but that scientists and scholars were thought to be the experts on how the term worked. That is, with the increasing prestige of science, people became used to using words whose exact meanings they did not need to know, because their exact meanings were left to the relevant scientific experts. . . . The result is that even ordinary users of the term "race" . . . thought of themselves as using a term whose value as a tool for speaking the truth was underwritten by the experts. (41)

John Carradine in *The Cosmic Man* is not unlike the foreigner, the immigrant, the undocumented worker, the nonwhite other who must erase himself and become white to thrive. He must learn how to perform whiteness. Thomas Elsaesser's work on immigrant Hollywood directors sheds some light on this supreme fiction of displacement. As Elsaesser asserts, "By repressing and disavowing their own homeland and heritage, they must have helped install at the heart of Hollywood an ambiguity regarding cultural identity that has typified the role of foreigners in Hollywood ever since" (99). Further,

> Is it not the immigrants, the "invaders," émigrés, and refugees who helped to make for all of the world, including the United States, out of Hollywood a country of the mind: the supreme fiction of displacement, transport and virtual realities? If the dream factory was thus partly "made in Europe," the worlds of make-believe, disavowal, deception, and self-deception have their own share of historical reality, fashioned from the contradictory triangulations of migration, national or ethnic stereotyping and exile. (121)

Whiteness thus depends on a disavowal of hybridity, an elimination of ethnicity, and an adherence to the othering mechanism of whiteness. It depends on correctly performing as white, but in the narrative of *The Cosmic Man* John Carradine's alien plays a ludic white who is also black. The film trades on what Peggy Phelan in *Unmarked* terms "the failure of racial difference to appear within the narrow range of the visible" (98). We simply do not know his race because we cannot see him—leading to the question posed by Phelan: "If racial difference is not registered visibly, where is it located? Is it a free floating signifier" (98)? How can the Cosmic Man secure whiteness, much less humanity? And are the two not immutably conflated?

Perhaps the most interesting transgressive film of the bad-white body is *The Thing with Two Heads*. In this film racist white scientist Dr. Maxwell Kirshner (Ray Milland) has a bad body: he has terminal cancer. His brain, however, is unaffected. Kirshner, wanting to avoid the inevitability of death, arranges to have his head transplanted onto the body of a man on death row. Only one candidate steps forward in time for the operation to be successful, and so, to save Kirshner's life, his head is grafted onto the body of African American prisoner Jack Moss (Roosevelt Grier). The two heads taunt one another, punch each other in the face, and exchange racist diatribes. One could view *The Thing with Two Heads* as a threat to white and black constructs; after all, if the two heads can live in one body, this forced coexistence potentially threatens the categories of both white and black. *The Thing with Two Heads* critiques and others white racism, but it also performs racism in the way that many "blaxploitation" films do. But *The Thing with Two Heads* disturbs the

FIGURE 13. Roosevelt Grier and Ray Milland are forced to coexist in the same body in *The Thing with Two Heads* (1972). Courtesy Jerry Ohlinger Archives.

myth of unsullied and totalized separate white and black cultures, even as it revels in their differences. In doing so, *The Thing with Two Heads* renders cultural diversity as dystopian and underscores the ideas expressed by Homi K. Bhabha: "Cultural diversity is also the representation of a radical rhetoric of the separation of totalized cultures that live unsullied by the intertextuality of their historical locations, safe in the Utopianism of a mythic memory of a unique collective identity" (34).

It is important to look at bad-white-body films such as *The Thing with Two Heads* through the lens of postmodernism because it makes terms like *bad* and *body* suspect. In addition, postmodernism does not demand allegiance to matters of so-called taste and aesthetics. A healthy postmodern questioning of the myths that these films explore suggests that we are in some ways dependent on such myths, as tools to aid us in examining routinely accepted—but generally unexamined—conventions. "The myths and conventions" recycled in popular culture, Hutcheon argues, "exist for a reason and postmodernism investigates that reason. The postmodern impulse is not to seek any total vision. It merely questions. If it finds such a vision, it questions how, in fact, it *made* it" (48).

CHAPTER FIVE

Performing the "Good" White

Whiteness as a construct depends on myths and distortions. What better place than the cinema to define, create, and maintain such myths and distortions? Since most cinema is essentially white cinema, most "good" women and "good" men are constructions of whiteness, as are "bad" women and "bad" men. The range of human experience is denied to nonwhites in a huge percentage of films. If to be human is to be white, it stands to reason that both goodness and badness are themselves categorically white in many circumstances. I am not suggesting that there are not numerous examples of on-screen performances of the good other or the bad other, but one must remember that cinema itself is largely a white space, and often the figure of the other is only used in service of what constitutes an other to whiteness. Most commercial American films and television series are still solidly performed and received as white. What happens when we mark these films and television programs as *white* constructions? What happens when we call them *white* films? After all, films with predominately black casts are called *black films* and in the past were called *race films*. Whiteness, if not questioned and marked, remains omnipresent yet manages to escape scrutiny within studies of race, class, gender, and sexuality in popular culture. White privilege in society and in the arts remains generally unchallenged, and the narratives and genres in which whiteness predominates remain unmarked. I find this state highly problematic. When one takes even the most cursory glance at cinema history, one is confronted with the predominating image of whiteness. Studies of black cinema, Native American cinema, African cinema, and blacks in white cinema abound. *Toms, Coons, Mulattoes, Mammies, and Bucks* by

Donald Bogle and other groundbreaking works by Manthia Diawara, Anna Everett, Rey Chow, Ella Shohat, Gina Marchetti, Jane Gaines, and others have all made significant progress toward understanding the way we view films in America today and toward examining the racist assumptions that audiences unconsciously make when they sit down to view a mainstream Hollywood film. Much has been written in the popular press about such films as *Pinky* (1949) and *Imitation of Life* (1934), about the star persona of Dorothy Dandridge, about blaxploitation and black spectatorship, and so on, but challenges against the unspoken yet utterly pervasive *whiteness* of cinema are generally limited in film studies.

Unfortunately, the other remains defined as "the problem" in public discussions of race. When the NAACP recently demanded that there be more and better representation of African Americans and Latinos on television, it was reported as "an issue" television producers (still largely white) should address. For most white audiences, executives, producers, directors, programmers, and advertisers, the underrepresentation of African Americans, Latinos, and other minorities is not a problem that they instinctively seek to correct. The white media power structure simply does not stand up and say, "We want better representation of people of all ethnicities." White audiences don't even *see* themselves as people of ethnicity; rather, they see themselves as unmarked and simply human, the normative audience against which all other viewers should be measured. All others are marked as problems, with the exception of sports figures and some comedians and mainstreamed actors, such as Denzel Washington, Tiger Woods, Whoopi Goldberg, Morgan Freeman, and a few other token figures in the cultural landscape. Clearly, this perspective has to change. Historically, African Americans are seen as "problem people," as Anna Everett notes. Hollywood, even in its stumbling efforts in the 1940s in so-called social-problem films, "did revisit issues of race and difference[;] . . . however in the main, these films once again construct African Americans on screen as the 'problem people,' instead of people confronting the problems of a racist society" (307). Obviously, as many critics have observed, these are white-centric films and remain more concerned with what whites think of African Americans than with African Americans themselves. What would happen if we turned this artificial paradigm around and saw *whites* as the problem? What happens when we specifically "white" genres (for example, white dance pictures, white westerns, white romances)?

Take, for example, *Holiday Inn* (1942), a white musical directed by Mark Sandrich, starring Bing Crosby, Fred Astaire, Marjorie Reynolds, and Virginia Dale. With the exception of perennial "mammy" Louise Beavers and her children, the cast is solidly white. The popular approach in current film criticism is to shift our gaze to Beavers, to note her otherness, and perhaps to critique her role as the black mammy figure, and so on. But where is the criticism of the *white* figures in musicals? It is essential that we examine the many white heterotopian fantasy narratives that perform and celebrate whiteness with tissue-thin plots and feature endless spectacles of white music and white people dancing. In white musicals, whiteness is celebrated in an almost totemic fashion, using shots of glowing back-lit white men and women dancing in a spectacle that is often fashioned to highlight the dazzling, shimmering, mirrored display of white bodies. I've always been intrigued by the utter mania, the frenzied insistence of the excitement in white musicals; performers in Busby Berkeley musicals and the later Arthur Freed musicals for MGM have simply "gotta dance," as Gene Kelly enthusiastically sings in *An American in Paris* (1951). An enormous amount of effort is expended in erasing the ethnic, working-class roots and African American influence on song and dance numbers in musicals, except when these numbers are performed as blackface routines, as was the case in a musical number in *Holiday Inn* dedicated to Abraham Lincoln, "who freed the slaves." To the obvious approval of the on-screen audience (nearly all musicals incorporate an on-screen audience as part of their performative structure), Crosby "corks it up" in a remarkably racist sequence as Beavers sings along appreciatively, albeit from the safe distance of the inn's kitchen. (Beavers's character, Mamie, may be able to cook the food the white folks eat, but she obviously isn't seen as being fit to socialize with them.) Yet perhaps some of the manic white performativity in mainstream musicals can be accounted for when we think about the work that white musicals had to do. White musicals, performers, and directors worked to create a suitable, identifiable screen presence for the typical American white viewer, erase or otherwise handle class differences that might arise, and, perhaps most astoundingly, obliterate any traces of the African American presence, influence, and/or body in the utterly synthetic white dance spectacles. As Toni Morrison argues, "Through significant and underscored omissions, startling contradictions, heavily nuanced conflicts through the way writers peopled their work with the signs and bodies of this presence—one

96

FIGURE 14. Ginger Rogers, Fred Astaire, and Bing Crosby inhabit an artificial world of performative white-ness in *Holiday Inn* (1942). Courtesy Jerry Ohlinger Archives.

can see that a real or fabricated Africanist presence was crucial to their sense of Americanness. And it shows" (6). White bodies are used to provide models of goodness or badness. In musicals the white bodies are often abstract, mechanized, heterosexual machines that exist only to serve the viewer. The disembodiedness of whiteness has its correlative in the embodiedness of "others." Mark Seltzer argues,

> These are the bodies-in-the-abstract that populate consumer and machine culture. But it is not merely that the privilege of relative disembodiment requires the more deeply embodied bodies (in consumer society: the female body, the racialized body, the working body) against which this privilege can be measured. Beyond that, it requires those more visibly embodied figures that, on the one side, epitomize the tensions between the typical and the individual and between the artifactual and the natural and, on the other, are the figures through which these tensions can be at once recognized and disrupted or disavowed. (64)

White bodies are abstracted, cut into pieces, used in discrete sections in white musicals, particularly in the Warner Brothers-Busby Berkeley musicals of the 1930s, where the human body was reduced to a mind-numbing series of endless smiles, well-shaped legs and breasts, white-blond heads, and restlessly toe-tapping feet, complimented by the manufactured grace of a series of anonymous yet immaculately attired white leading men. White musicals provide a utopian space to deploy whiteness. "Tales and legends seem to have the same role. They are deployed, like games, in a space outside of and isolated from daily competition, that of the past, the marvelous, the original. In that space can thus be revealed, dressed as gods or heroes, the models of good or bad ruses that can be used every day" (de Certeau 23).

In *Holiday Inn* Bing Crosby and Fred Astaire are models of good whiteness. Good whiteness is straight and interested in the "girl." The female object of desire is at the center of this thin romantic triangle. Performative whiteness needs continual visual and aural reinforcement to ensure its existence and to fight against the essential instability of whiteness as a socialized construct. We see endless close-ups of adoring white faces, white legs dancing, white torsos twisting, the whole white body engaged in performing itself. White musicals engage in what Laura Marks terms "sense envy." They display "the desire of one culture for the sensory knowledge of another" (239). The sense of a lack of restraint, of a body in movement displaying sexuality, is intimately associated with ethnicity, especially black culture, Jewish culture, and working-class vaudeville cultures in the minds of mainstream viewers. In *Holiday Inn* these gestures are appropriated and flattened out, whitened in a sanitizing of spectacle. Colonialism depends on spectacle to exercise its hegemony. "The society that brings the spectacle into being does not dominate underdeveloped regions solely through the exercise of economic hegemony. It also dominates them in its capacity *as the society of the spectacle*" (Debord 37). That same hegemony works to define subjectivity itself as white. Blackness is omitted, and last names are altered to erase ethnicities that would highlight Jewishness, Native Americanness, and the traces of other ethnicities. As Diana Fuss points out in her study of Frantz Fanon, colonial projects deny subjectivity to the other.

> Fanon implicitly disputes his own initial formula . . . [and] asks whether, in colonial regimes of representation, even otherness may be appropriated exclusively by white subjects. Fanon considers the possibility that colonialism may inflict its greatest psychical violence precisely by attempting to exclude blacks from the very self-other dynamic that makes subjectivity possible. (142)

Whenever otherness may be appropriated by white subjects and white films, especially musicals, romances, and melodramas, it can be used to raise the specter of class difference, if only to solve (and thus erase) that difference with the tidy ending of the films, usually uniting or marrying two white figures from different classes, who can then *class pass* in society through marriage, elopement, or other plot contrivances. Most striking about this class-passing scenario is its ceaseless repetition, its continual reperformance to reinforce a blatantly fraudulent construct. But as bell hooks argues, "Racial solidarity, particularly the solidarity of whiteness, has historically always been used to obscure class, to make the white poor see their interests as one with the world of white privilege. Similarly, the black poor have always been told that class can never matter as much as race" (*Where We Stand* 5).

Class is also problematic in *Let's Dance* (1950), a Fred Astaire and Betty Hutton white musical in which Hutton plays Kitty McNeil, a good-white mother who wishes to shield her son from her wealthy and privileged great-grandmother. Good-white-hoofer Donald Elwood (Astaire) falls for Kitty, and the two dance and sing their way out of their class-based problem. Astaire, as usual, is cast as the amiable white fellow who may not be born to privilege but can surely charm his way to class privilege. His famous "Piano Dance" number is the ostensible highlight of the film, allowing the white moviegoer to stop thinking about the class problem and escape into a pleasurable world of fantasy. Jackie Stacey, in her study of female spectatorship, *Star Gazing*, defines escapism as "associated with leaving behind one's own life and participating in another imaginary world for a short period of time" (116). The British white women Stacey studied spoke frankly about their ability to fantasize when watching Hollywood spectacles in the 1930s and 1940s.

> It was something completely different to what my life was. I used to put myself in their place, pretend for an hour or two. . . . I wasn't attractive or had a good figure, I wore glasses and didn't have any money to buy glamorous clothes and the cinema was escapism away from a rather dull life. . . . [I enjoyed] the usually happy crowd—the cinemas were always full—and the special "Saturday night out" kind of excitement—of living in another more glamorous kind of life for a few hours. (116)

Fantasy gives audiences a space in which to play with their own subjectivity, to explore their own fluid senses of selves, as they are performed and rehearsed across real and fictional constructs of whiteness. This pleasurable space allows the spectator to enjoy a type of class-passing that can exist in the space between fantasy and reality. "The significance of such fantasy worlds is also, importantly, written about in relation to the spectator's own worlds, in many cases a world of wartime or postwar austerity, routine and lacking glamour. It is the difference between these worlds that produces the fascination and the desire for movement from one to the other" (Stacey 117).

One of the greatest performers who effectively embodied the fantasy figure of female white goodness was Mary Pickford. Few are aware that the high point in the history of cinema for women producers and directors was in the early, pioneering days, when it was not unusual to find scores of women as active behind the camera as they were in front of the camera. Mary Pickford was one of a host of strong pioneering white women producers, directors, and writers, such as Lois Weber, Frances Marion, Mabel Normand, Dorothy Davenport Reid, and many others, who wielded a tremendous amount of power and influence in the motion picture industry. Pickford was known, in fact, to control every facet of her

FIGURE 15. Mary Pickford (center of frame), the little girl who wasn't allowed to grow up, in *Pollyanna* (1920). Courtesy Jerry Ohlinger Archives.

own career with an iron hand. She almost single-handedly began the "star system," insisting that she be credited for her performances, for example. When audiences began to recognize her name in the credits, she developed an unprecedented and unparalleled following.

Pickford was also well known for her business acumen; indeed, the financially astute Charlie Chaplin called her the "Bank of America's Sweetheart" (qtd. in Acker 54). In contract negotiations with Adolph Zukor's Famous Players Co. in 1916, for example, Pickford told Zukor flatly, "I simply can't afford to work for only ten thousand dollars a week" (qtd. in Acker 54). Pickford was, after all, voted the "Number 1 Actress of the Year" in *Photoplay* fifteen times in a row and eventually went on to claim a peak salary of three hundred thousand dollars per picture. Surprisingly, Pickford claimed that she never attended school and learned to read from painstakingly deciphering billboards, but she seemed to have an intuitive grasp of her value as a fantasy figure of Victorian femininity. It is a telling irony that the woman who played the role of the archetypal virgin (she was known as the "Great Unkissed") was, in life, a perfect example of the independent New Woman: athletic, financially independent, and sexually strident.

Well into adulthood, Mary Pickford was still forced by the public to play a young girl. To her increasing dismay, Pickford found that her fans would not accept her as an adult woman. She wore flat shoes, stood in specially designed pits on the set, and bound her breasts to create the façade of perpetual childhood. She was often cast against tall men to foster the illusion of adolescence, and by the end of her career as a "juvenile," producers were forced to use oversized chairs, carpets, rooms, and other props to maintain the illusion of youth. Mary Pickford thus leaves an enigmatic legacy. She is emblematic of the pioneering early New Woman, strong and able to build a fortune and have almost complete control over her life and her image. Yet Pickford almost exclusively played the part of the virginal white girl-child, an image that worked against the rising image of the New Woman. Pickford was often placed in situations in which she was the underdog, the orphan, or the motherless child in search of a father figure. But in life she was quite capable of fending for herself. She made 201 movies in her career, which spanned a quarter of a century, but she remained, in the eyes of her admirers, the eternal symbol of white young girlhood. Indeed, one might well argue that Mary Pickford, in catering to the demands of her white audience, influenced the entire course of the dominant cinema with her iconic portrayals of the unsullied white heroine, a racial stereotype that persists to this day.

Comedy, as in *The Mating Season* (1951), can serve to offer a pleasurable space to negotiate fantasies of white class mobility. Comedy "is available to women and all oppressed people as a weapon with which to express their aggression . . . [and] emphasizes an impulse toward *renewal* and *social transformation*" (Rowe 102). In *The Mating Season* socialite Maggy Carleton (Gene Tierney) marries working man Val McNulty (John Lund), who is mortified when his lower-class mother, Ellen McNulty (Thelma Ritter) appears on the scene and is immediately mistaken for a servant. Even though the film's comedic structure smooths over the edges of white class difference, *The Mating Season* explores class as an indeterminate marker.

As examined in *The Mating Season* and other comedies of this type, class-passing is one of the more interesting, yet frequently ignored, tropes of American cinema. Rita Felski asserts, "A person from a lower-class background who has acquired education and money might be said to pass as middle or upper class in the same way as a gay man or lesbian can pass as straight" (38). Class passing is in some ways like race-passing, gender-passing, or straight/gay-passing, but class-passing, like whiteness, is not often noticed or examined. It is essentially viewed as normative behavior, especially in America, where one is expected to do as much class-passing as possible, regardless of one's race, gender, or economic circumstances. Nothing is more unsettling, it seems, than someone who is actually wealthy, well educated, or "well bred" but who refuses to perform his or her class "correctly." Hetty Green, the "Witch of Wall Street," who made and loaned millions of dollars to numerous financial institutions, defiantly refused to "act the part" of the rich businesswoman, dressing in rags and eating table scraps (Hetty Green). Such behavior continues to fascinate the general American public. Flaunting wealth, whether we actually attain it or purchase the appearance of it through credit, is the accepted norm of the American consumer. Whites are trained by television commercials, magazine promotions, radio spots, internet "spam," and web "banner" advertisements to be good consumers, as are people of all ethnicities. Whiteness is a commodity that can be bought and faked; and, to perform whiteness correctly, increasingly one is expected to be a gluttonous American consumer.

The allure of whiteness is one of the principal commodities of the American cinema; it is a spectacle that assists in stabilizing the representation of whiteness as a social construct. In early American cinema white-ness was all there was to see. There were, of course, occasional black "nov-elty" shorts and Edison's films of Native Americans performing ceremo-nial dances in his primitive studio, the Black Maria, but for the most part early cinema was a celebration of white privilege. The white woman glows, as she does in both the silent and sound cinema, because of film stock, special filters, backlighting, and a blast of light from above. After shooting the master shot of a scene, it is still customary to "light the woman" out of the master shot first and to make her single shot, or close-up, as attractive and as carefully composed as possible. In the dominant cinema such deference is motivated solely by practicality: the woman's makeup will "run" under the lights much more quickly than the man's, and care must be taken to get her best possible physical appearance on film. But class difference is also marked by color in cinematography. "A middle- or upper-class aristocratic woman's face might be rendered nearly as white as the paper on which it was printed or the screen on which it was projected, while working-class men would be even darker than work-ing-class women" (Dyer, *White* 113).

Class issues erupt in another all-white comedy, *The Philadelphia Story* (1940), with Cary Grant, Katharine Hepburn, James Stewart, Ruth Hussey, Henry Daniell, and Hillary Brooke. In *The Philadelphia Story* "society girl" Tracy Samantha Lord (Hepburn) yearns for a more down-to-earth romance, one associated with the working class. Cary Grant plays her ex-husband, C. K. Dexter Haven, and James Stewart plays a fast-talk-ing, working-class reporter, Macaulay ("call me Mike") Connor, who falls for Hepburn. Here, the mechanism of class-passing is used to present working-classed sexuality and contrast it with upper-classed chasteness and boredom. Somehow the emergence of the triumphant couple trumps class, as if romance always trumps class, and marrying is always about marrying "up." Hepburn, through her brief romantic involvement with Stewart, raises both members of the couple to a higher-class stratum.

Perhaps one of the finest examples of a white musical that openly deals with class issues is the spectacle *Gold Diggers of 1933* (1933). The heroines, who are all good girls but who are nevertheless out of work because of the Depression, are Carol King (Joan Blondell), Trixie Lor-raine (Aline MacMahon), Fay Fortune (Ginger Rogers), and Polly Parker (Ruby Keeler). Brad Roberts/Robert Treat Bradford (played by Dick Powell), who has a crush on Polly, is the good-white-male figure, a

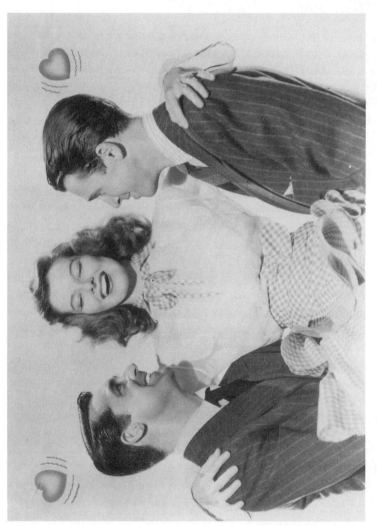

FIGURE 16. *Left to right:* Cary Grant, Katharine Hepburn, and James Stewart form the classic white love triangle in *The Philadelphia Story* (1940). Courtesy Jerry Ohlinger Archives.

wealthy composer who is class-passing as a working man in an effort to convince his snobbish Boston family that he can make a living on his own, writing music for the theater. When producer Barney Hopkins (Ned Sparks) suddenly needs money to put on a new musical, Brad comes to the rescue, but not before his brother, J. Lawrence Bradford (Warren William, one of the great unsung white villains of the American cinema), learns of Brad's involvement with both Polly and the show and travels to New York, with the family attorney, Faneul H. Peabody (Guy Kibbee) in tow, to put an end to their relationship. However, J. Lawrence Bradford mistakes Carol for Polly, and Carol plays along with the mistaken identity both to keep the show afloat and to protect Brad and Polly. Trixie Lorraine, however, seems only to be out for herself and tries to bleed money out of Peabody and Bradford. Mervyn LeRoy directed the film's convoluted narrative, but Busby Berkeley's dance numbers are entirely his own creation, at once bizarre and mind-numbing. White women's bodies in musicals, such as *Gold Diggers of 1933,* reduce the female form "to biotic tile in an abstract mosaic that is not devoid of overtones of power" (Fischer, *Shot* 138). This intense mechanization of white bodies usually manages to deflect class issues, but the songs and narrative of *Gold Diggers of 1933* constantly remind the audience of the desperate circumstances of most people in the Depression. The finale, "Remember My Forgotten Man," is a paean to the forgotten men of World War I, then standing in bread lines, dreaming of jobs, homes, food, and the restoration of their human dignity. What makes "Remember My Forgotten Man" doubly unusual is its positioning within the film's narrative; it comes at the end of the film, and there is no counternarrative to bookend it or soften its message. For what is mostly a light and essentially frothy film, despite its racist and classist subtext, the somber melody of "Remember My Forgotten Man" is an anomaly, a socially responsible musical number. I should note, however, that the film appropriates black choral music to signify poverty and strife and uses harmonic structures from African American blues and spiritual music. *Gold Diggers of 1933* is an exemplification of bell hooks's assertion that "race and gender can be used as screens to deflect attention away from the harsh realities class politics exposes" (*Where We Stand* 7). Poverty is raced, so that white participants and audiences can both engage in and deflect themselves from the harsh realities of the Great Depression. Despite the Depression, white women have exchange value

106

FIGURE 17. The white female body as an article of commerce in *Gold Diggers of 1933* (1933). Courtesy Jerry Ohlinger Archives.

in the sexual arena, and the spectacle of the white musical affords them an opportunity to display that wealth and to temporarily escape their liminal class situation. In *Gold Diggers of 1933* white women act as fantasy figures to deflect class difference, even if within the film's narrative they constantly have to deal with problems of financial instability, unpaid bills, sexual harassment, lack of clothing, food, makeup, and associated concerns. *Gold Diggers of 1933* falsely remedies class difficulties by eliding them with the heterotopian coupling of various white men and women. As in most musicals, identification shifts are typically abrupt; one minute the women are bitterly cursing their lack of good fortune, and the next minute they are happily belting out a tune, either as recreation (to amuse each other) or for the benefit of an audience.

The liminal quality of identity in musicals is one of the factors viewers into the spectacle. In 1981 Herbert Ross's film of Dennis Potter's postmodern musical *Pennies from Heaven* returned to the Depression era's format of the white musical to demonstrate the reality gap created by a series of relentlessly cheerful musical numbers as they are interspersed with the narrative of the pathetic existence of the film's protagonist, starving sheet-music salesman Arthur Parker (Steve Martin). Clearly, *Pennies from Heaven* aspires to be as troubling and phantasmal as *Gold Diggers of 1933*, but in the artificially robust American economy of the 1980s, the film seemed out of place and thus failed to connect with audiences, who simply couldn't identify with Arthur Parker's plight.

If, as Mary Ann Doane suggests, "whiteness in its symbolic dimension . . . is a form of masquerade which conceals an identity" (229), what does this masquerade suggest about white audiences and their constructions as good or bad? How do white audiences perform good whiteness or bad whiteness? Much has been written about cinema audiences in general, exploring the relationship between the construct of the film being witnessed and the gender and class of moviegoers, yet little reception theory has been written about white audience behavior. Audiences are often assumed to be largely white, but considerable evidence exists to suggest that, in the glory days of Hollywood, blacks attended all-white Hollywood films and that whites attended all-black-cast films. Everett in *Returning the Gaze* studies the extensive writings about white- and black-cast films by African Americans. Manthia Diawara has done important work on black spectators, as has Jacqueline Bobo.

White women were often constructed as bad audiences or bad movie-goers. As Shelley Stamp observes, "the recurring figure of a boisterous, talkative woman" (27) was popular in the silent era and "chatty women became one of the more familiar caricatures of the era" (26). Miriam Hansen notes in *Babel and Babylon* that "'the rule of silence' had to be learned in the 1910s" (95). "Women were needed as consumers" (Staiger 179) in the developing cinema, but the role of white female spectatorship was both objectifying and subjectifying.

> What the culture taught them was that their social and public opportunities for mobility and participation were permissible, even desirable, for deter-mining a New Woman who could serve consumer culture. It was no simple coincidence that the social phenomenon of cinema invited women to find pleasure in their bodies and experience unrestrained passions while it simul-taneously constructed them as the object of (male) desire and of immature emotions that needed to be tamed and controlled. This double-edged process of subjectivity and objectification was fundamental to recuperating female desire so that it could function in the service of patriarchy. (Rabi-novitz 185)

The good-white woman as a consumer of motion pictures was thus both free and contained. Thorstein Veblen dubbed the New Woman "the most ridiculous production of modern times," adding,

> She is petted, and is permitted, or even required, to consume largely and conspicuously—vicariously for her husband or other natural guardian. She is exempted, or debarred, from vulgarly useful employment—in order to perform leisure vicariously for the good repute of her natural (pecuniary) guardian. These offices are the conventional marks of the un-free. (218)

The white woman was, then, largely constructed as a consumer of images. Consequently, there was much anxiety on the part of theatrical film exhibitors because of the class differences among women. Exhibitors wished to appeal to all classes while *appearing* to privilege the upper-class woman. Special seats were set aside for "ladies" in a Jim Crow-style arrangement; "ladies," of course, meant white women, and the seating separated them by class. "Class-conscious women were thereby guaran-teed that they would constitute a significant body of the audience and perhaps more important, that they would not have to rub elbows with less cultivated patrons who might also be in attendance" (Stamp 14). While the "[u]nreal unity the [on-screen] spectacle proclaims *masks* the class divisions on which real unity of the capitalist mode is based" (Debord 46), the off-screen space both encouraged white class prejudice and encouraged good (read *silent*) female behavior. The "genteel culture of female moviegoing promoted by the industry accomplished much more than simply encouraging patronage among this desirable segment of the market. Such promotions also guided women's expectations, furnishing them with clues about how to conduct themselves in picture houses" (Stamp 15). White women were thus being used as colonized figures of commerce while simultaneously allowing themselves to be further colonized by social-conduct guides. They were mocked for being loud and praised for being poised, quiet, white, and genteel. Good-white women were, therefore, subject as spectators to the dualities usually associated with the Victorian age. "Woman, Victorian society dictated, was to be chaste, delicate, and loving. . . . She was seen, that is, as being both higher and lower, both innocent and animal, pure yet quintessentially sexual" (Smith-Rosenberg 183). Performing good-white femininity meant shutting up and removing large hats, so it is perhaps contrary to expectations that many women filmgoers actually preferred action and spectacle. "In fact, women were attracted to sexually explicit, action-oriented, and agitational films that encouraged alternative viewing modes and extratextual engagement at a time when filmmaking was increasingly standardized toward classical norms" (Stamp 198). Thus, despite exhibitor expectations, women who were privileged, white, and gentile were invited into cinemas to provide respectability to exhibition houses, yet they made a great deal of noise and liked action-adventure films, especially serials, which often featured female action heroines.

But to be a good audience in dominant white culture increasingly meant to be a quiet audience. Unfortunately, this call for silence meant that many black audiences, who had a propensity to interact with the films they viewed in a call-and-response mode, were coded by white people as poorly behaved: only in all-black theaters could African Americans or others feel free to respond to films as they wished. Ironically, with the rise of role-playing video games in the late 1990s, exhibitors are beginning to realize that audiences desire a more interactive moving-image experience. Since the early 1950s, home television audiences have been shouting answers to the screen and cheering on contestants during such quiz shows as *The $64,000 Question* and *21*. In Japan television audiences can now interact with game shows and play them in real time at home by using sophisticated remote-control devices, and these viewers win prizes just as valuable as those given to the on-screen contestants. A recent study of American soldiers connects loud and boisterous cinema interaction with an all-male environment. In such an environment male spectators could be as unruly as they wished. William Friedman Fagelson notes that, during World War II, "Theatre mangers found audiences the rowdiest in their memory: they howled, hissed, and booed at pictures, demanded Westerns, carved their initials on seats, sometimes even fired buckshot at the screen" (95). Fagelson notes that soldiers sometimes developed a complicated view of Hollywood films that whitewashed the home front and portrayed war inaccurately. Aboard troop ships, where films were screened in 16mm format on deck at night, "inventive participatory activities arose" (95) away from the confining theaters at home. Men wolf-whistled at attractive women who appeared on-screen and interjected remarks throughout screenings. These audiences, as Fagelson notes, defied the ideal of silent, passive receivers of film texts. The responsive women viewers described above also cast doubt on the model, as do African American audiences. But a good audience remains defined as a silent, almost reverent audience, a construct that is deeply related to class, race, and gender. The quietest audiences are those that attend films at museums and retro houses, where all comments during a film are met with a stern glance and admonitions to remain silent. Happily, there are exceptions to this rule of silence in the cathedral of cinema. These "exceptional screenings," in which audiences are active and vocal participants during the viewing of a film, break the fourth wall of cinema reception. Audiences who are exiled from one another, silenced by the unseen panoptic presence, enact an agreed-upon definition of good-spectator behavior. Thus good spectatorship is nonparticipatory, silent, and white.

Indeed, performing the good-white male proves impossible for the closeted male in a military environment in Claire Denis's *Beau Travail* (1999). *Beau Travail* scrutinizes the performative white body as a site of discipline and conflicting desire. In many ways *Beau Travail*, with its vintage Benjamin Britten score and its lengthy sequences of ritualistic calisthenics, can be seen as a sort of "male musical," in which the performing bodies of men, trapped in the French Foreign Legion, find simultaneous liberation and social agency in the harshest of regimes. As Agnès Godard, the film's cinematographer, noted, "[T]he most inexhaustible landscapes for me remain faces and bodies" (qtd. in Vincentelli 166). These "inexhaustible" possibilities for performing the homoeroticized male body are remarkable in *Beau Travail,* a tale told in aesthetic shots of male bodies. "The abstraction," said Claire Denis, "was in the meeting of the landscape and the rules, and all those bodies doing the same thing" (qtd. in Taubin 126).

Jim Hoberman notes that "in its hypnotic ritual, *Beau Travail* suggests a John Ford cavalry western interpreted by Marguerite Duras" ("Work" 121). It is a film that relies on memory-editing techniques, memories of bodies sutured together by the voice-over of the central protagonist, Galoup. And it is a film that relies on performances rendered through the subjective re-membered gaze of a narrator whose mental landscape is rife with homoeroticized images of faces and bodies. *Beau Travail* is loosely based on Herman Melville's allegorical novella *Billy Budd, Foretopman,* set in 1797 in the British Royal Navy. The original is an account of an innocent sailor, Billy Budd, who is destroyed by a petty officer, John Claggart. Director Claire Denis also draws upon the Benjamin Britten opera *Billy Budd.* Both sources are key in their homoeroticism, which is tied to danger, isolation, and injustice. Claire Denis sets the story in the French Foreign Legion. The Billy Budd character, Gilles Sentain, is played by Grégoire Colin. Colin is muscular, lithe, and attractive, and he captures the attention of the commanding officer, Bruno Forestier (Michel Subor). Intriguingly, Subor also appeared in Jean-Luc Godard's classic film *Le Petit soldat* (1963) as a character—also named Bruno Forestier—who is attempting to fight against France's involvement in the racist war in Algeria. Godard's film was summarily banned by the Gaullist government and has only recently been made available to the public. In *Beau Travail* Denis Lavant plays the Claggart-like villain and central narrator, Galoup, who appears to be in love with Bruno Forestier and jealous of newcomer Sentain. Galoup's jealousy destroys him, and it is this self-ruination that we watch in a rather complicated flashback, subjective, point-of-view narrative, punctuated by Galoup's voice-over as he reads from his diary and retraces his voyage of self-destruction and removal from the legion. "Maybe freedom begins with remorse," he writes. Indeed, the ambiguous ending suggests that Galoup may ultimately escape a prison of performing heterosexuality and performing the life of the exiled legionnaire as he dances to the strains of the classic gay anthem, "The Rhythm of the Night" by Corona.

Beau Travail has very little dialogue; in this characteristic it has more in common with dance or opera than with narrative film. It is punctuated by highly stylized, repetitive performances of ritual behavior in the confines of the all-male, multiethnic French Foreign Legion. The manner in which Denis introduces the men suggests that they are indeed wordless performative vehicles of masculine acts. In one of the first of many drills we watch from above, the men shimmy across the desert floor like lizards beneath barbed wire. We see many bare male upper bodies, often through the objectifying gaze of Galoup's flashbacks and fantasies. Indeed, because the tale is told through Galoup's subjective imagination, an imagination that is clearly informed by homophobia and denial of his own sexuality, we are forced into the subjectivity of a closeted homosexual who is an embodiment of excess and desire. This has a disorienting and uncomfortable effect. In addition, our narrator is completely lacking in objectivity. He is so consumed with jealousy and self-loathing that he can only share with us his tortured and sensual memories. As the camera pans along men's chests and beautiful faces, we share Galoup's subjectivity as we share his confusion. We share in the objectification of male bodies as much as we share in the aestheticization of their performances of masculinity and desire.

After a long, wordless introduction to the men performing tai chi, the camera stops on Galoup. He is the only one of all the men squeezed into the frame who is clearly gazing at the men in adoration. He begins to read from his diary. After being thrown out of the legion—deemed "unfit for life"—he is now in Marseilles. The use of voice-over and the intimacy with which Galoup reads his diary also push the audience further into a joined subjectivity with Galoup. "Unfit for civil life," he repeats, like a character out of *Hiroshima mon amour* (1959). In a highly stylized shot he remembers a naked man swimming underwater. Through memory editing, his reverie is interrupted by the face of his obsession, his superior, Commandant Bruno Forestier. But he immediately associates Forestier with Gilles Sentain, and the performance of a homoerotic love triangle begins, as does jealousy. "I felt something vague and menacing take hold of me," he says, as he thinks about Sentain. In his memories Galoup sees the men perform a balletic series of maneuvers. The camera tracks along with the men as they perform various drills, in a scene rife with homoeroticism and unexpressed bodily desire.

Almost sotto voce, in the style of *Le Petit soldat,* Galoup sings words from the legionnaire's theme song, "Loving one's superior, obeying him, that's the essence of our tradition." Ironically, we know that Galoup will disobey the will of the law and his beloved Forestier when he arranges for the murder of Sentain. Galoup is carefully constructed as an exile. He can never really belong to the Foreign Legion because he is humanized by his erotic attachments. Humanization runs counter to the mechanization of the performing male bodies of the war machine. That Galoup is not demonized in the manner in which Claggart is demonized in Melville's novel is interesting. He is instead seen as a pathetic, grotesque outsider. For example, in a scene in which the soldiers perform a simulated siege of an abandoned building, Galoup is emotionally and physically removed from the others by camera movement and shot composition.

It is primarily through performativity and exchanges of gaze that we begin to see that Galoup is infatuated with Bruno Forestier. Galoup is utterly closeted and unable to face the fact that he is deeply in love with his superior. As he obsessively cleans and irons we hear him reminisce about Forestier in his voice-over. "Bruno. Bruno Forestier. I feel so alone when I think of my superior. I respected him a lot. I liked him." *I liked him* seems like an unusual phrase given the militaristic environs. In his gestures and behavior it is clear that Galoup lives to please Forestier. We see a photograph of the young Forestier. Galoup tells us, "A rumor dogged him after the Algerian War. He never confided in me." Gradually, we come to understand that Forestier has been the subject of rumors of homosexuality. Indeed, in Galoup's flashbacks Forestier behaves very much in keeping with an aesthete who loves to gaze at his own men. Forestier's performance of homosexuality is glimpsed only briefly but is nonetheless apparent. He, like Galoup, spends much time carefully combing his hair and grooming himself in a mirror before he greets his men. Coupled with his longing, languorous, erotic looks at the men, it becomes clear that Forestier is quite comfortable aestheticizing his beautiful men.

Galoup says of Forestier, "I admired him without knowing why." Perhaps this statement can be read as a growing recognition and acceptance of their shared homosexuality. Yet this thought is broken by anger and the memory of an unreciprocated love. "He knew I was a perfect Legionnaire. And he didn't give a damn." Again Galoup repeats the name: "Bruno, Bruno Forestier." Galoup is a man without a country, a man without a clearly defined sexuality, and a man without a family. Family is the promise of the Foreign Legion, but Galoup is not welcomed or loved by his superior or even by his own men. He follows them on their night off in the city, as if desiring to share in their camaraderie. He has given himself to the legion, but he cannot contain his desires and longs for the homosocial bonds shared by his men. He is mad with jealousy. He is also jealous of his superior, but he still does not know why. His memories demonstrate exactly why. His memories inhabit a landscape of homoerotic performances enjoyed by the clearly homosexual gaze of Forestier.

A trenchant example of these vague, subjective memories presents itself to the audience in the form of a knife fight, gorgeously simulated underwater and saturated with the display of the beautiful musculature of naked men. A flashback cuts to a shot of Forestier lounging on his side, smoking, clearly entranced by the visual display of homoerotic performativity. And in Galoup's memory he is suddenly made aware of his intense jealousy for Sentain. "Sentain seduced everyone. He attracted stares. People were attracted to his calmness, his openness. Deep down I felt a sort of rancor, a rage brimming." This rage is connected to Galoup's feelings of sexual inadequacy and insecurity about his rough appearance. Stuart Klawans describes him as "a homely veteran (dog face on top of fireplug body)" (34). In contrast, Sentain—Grégoire Colin—*is* beautiful; even after an enforced head shaving, he is a beautiful young man with rather lush, large eyes and a large mouth. After Sentain captures the eye of Forestier, Galoup decides to murder Sentain. His flashbacks here are punctuated by objectified performing male bodies in various postures, formations, and drills. We see Galoup and Sentain face off in a circular fashion like animals sniffing one another's scent. Here, the Britten score crashes in an otherwise quiet setting, underscored by the natural sound of the waves lapping at the shore. This performance is clearly a fantasy sequence rather than a memory, and the narrative returns to find Galoup forcing Sentain to punch him. Sentain is punished by being sent out into the desert with a broken compass. When that compass is later found, Forestier informs Galoup that he will be court-martialed. "Your Legion days are over." Amazingly, Sentain survives.

Back in France, Galoup, even in civilian clothing, is unable to stop performing as a legionnaire. He spends what seems like an endless amount of time obsessively cornering his sheets in military fashion. Wordlessly, he pulls out a gun and places it on his muscled torso. He fondly remembers his men as we see a tattoo on his skin: "Serve the good cause and die." As he fondles the gun, we flash cut to a final fantasy sequence in which he dances to "The Rhythm of the Night," and we are left with a typically ambiguous Denis ending in which "maybe freedom begins with remorse." It is only after leaving the legion that Galoup allows himself to engage in a fantasy that seems to embrace his homosexuality.

This final scene, read within the context of performance theory, allows for a recontextualization of Galoup's sexual identity. Galoup may indeed be reperforming his body in a scene of agency, which allows him to escape the confines of a white body that has been imprisoned in the homoerotic yet homophobic French Foreign Legion. This is a considerably different ending and message from any found in Melville's *Billy Budd*. The gap between our understanding of Galoup's memories and his own seeming inability to understand those same flashbacks leaves a space for the many repetitive and stylized performances of male bodies in battle with and in context with masculinity, desire, and "homosociality." That gap is the abstract space of the possibility of agency through white performativity.

CHAPTER SIX

PERFORMING THE "BAD" WHITE

Bad-white women are almost always good underneath, but bad-white men are just plain *bad*. As a general rule, bad-white men are born bad or reared badly. Thus male white badness is clearly connected to inadequate white motherhood. Bad-white men often get that way because they have bad-white mothers, at least according to the logic of white movies. On the other hand, bad-white women's hidden goodness is quite often hidden and later connected to white motherhood or, in the case of prostitutes, a kind of sexual motherhood—thus the cliché of the hooker with a heart of gold. Badness and goodness are, then, like whiteness, connected to reproduction and women's use value as reproducers of the white race. Quite often, the bad/good-white woman's ability to properly reproduce and mother is complicated by class issues, as in the case of the maternal melodrama cycle.

The white maternal melodrama centers on maternal suffering, class strife, and the wages of infidelity. The white woman's separation from her white child because of illicit unions and forbidden love is portrayed as the ultimate punishment for white women. The white child is more valuable than the white woman. This is a given. One title that captures this phenomenon is *The Most Precious Thing in Life* (1934). A white woman who sacrifices a child, for whatever reason, is always punished on-screen, providing white women in the audience with an exemplar of the social code and allowing them to feel her pain and to enjoy her punishment.

In *Forbidden* (1932), for example, Lulu Smith (Barbara Stanwyck) is a good-white woman who goes bad when she falls in love with a married attorney, Bob Grover (Adolphe Menjou). Stanwyck's character, marked as good and virginal by her spinster-schoolteacher status, takes a cruise, during which she falls for Menjou's character, a smooth-talking villain who fails to reveal that he is already married. After Bob's deception is discovered, he sets up Lulu in a "love nest." When Lulu has Bob's child out of wedlock, she allows Bob to adopt the baby, so that the child can enjoy the privileges of an upper-class white home. Bob's wife, Helen (Dorothy Peterson), is unable to have children because she's a quadriplegic bound to a wheelchair: the "barren" white woman. Helen's inability to reproduce lessens her whiteness. Notably, she is often shot in darkness, while Lulu, with her ability to reproduce, is shot in high-key lighting. Lulu is the good/bad-white woman who must suffer in silence, watch her child as he is raised by others, and stand by in silence as her lover runs for governor.

Forbidden is a familiar variant on *Back Street,* first filmed in 1932 and remade in 1941 and 1961. *Back Street* is based on a popular novel written by Fannie Hurst. Irene Dunne, Margaret Sullavan, and Susan Hayward have all played the fallen white woman of the film, the androgynously named Ray Schmidt (Rae Smith, in the two later versions), whose love for a married man threatens white heterocentric society. Ray/Rae is coded by darkness and shadows, which are associated with negativity and sin in a racially coded and racially lit celluloid universe. White women in maternal melodramas and in fallen-woman films are thus trapped by their own whiteness. As Jeanine Basinger contends, "[T]hese stories are about [white] women who have no one to help them" (394). White femaleness is, finally, a trap.

Madame X (1937) is another revealing example of the maternal melodrama. Gladys George plays a woman who sacrifices herself in this genuinely moving film directed by Sam Wood. Attorney Bernard Fleuriot (Warren William) is the unforgiving white husband who throws his wife, Jacqueline Fleuriot (Gladys George), out into the street when she is unfaithful to him. Bernard sees to it that Jacqueline is permanently separated from their son, Raymond (John Beal), who grows up to be a lawyer, just like his father. In the film's climax, in a twist of fate possible only in the movies, Raymond ends up as the pro-bono defense counsel for a pathetic white female creature who, unknown to him, is his mother. She has been reduced to destitute homelessness and alcoholism and is blackmailed by the despicable LeRocle (Henry Daniell), who seeks to use her past identity to disgrace Bernard Fleuriot, her husband. Jacqueline shoots LeRocle and goes on trial for murder but refuses to defend herself for fear

FIGURE 18. Jacqueline Fleuriot (Gladys George), defended by the son who does not know her (John Beal, *second from left*) during the climactic murder trial of *Madame X* (1937). Courtesy Jerry Ohlinger Archives.

that her real identity will be discovered. Raymond, who defends her without knowing that she is his mother, cannot understand her unwillingness to defend herself. Jacqueline would rather go to the guillotine than let her son know that his mother is a fallen woman, a white woman who was unfaithful to his father. Her husband, Bernard, finally realizes the true identity of the defendant, who conveniently dies before sentence can be passed; the film suggests that Bernard will spend the rest of his life repenting his hard-heartedness. As with *Back Street, Madame X* was a much-filmed property; first produced as a silent film in 1916 starring Dorothy Donnelly, there were subsequent versions in 1920 (with Pauline Frederick), 1929 (Ruth Chatterton), 1966 (Lana Turner), and most recently in 1981 (as a television movie with Tuesday Weld). Old tropes, like old legends, defy the passage of time, and the tale of the sacrificed mother continues to serve as useful fodder for contemporary audiences.

A central motif of the white maternal melodrama is the sacrifice that a mother makes when she does not reveal her identity to the child from whom she is separated. The tension, of course, arises whenever the two are near. In *The Sin of Madelon Claudet* (1931) Helen Hayes's character becomes a prostitute to support her son. She sends him to medical school, but she never reveals to him that she is his mother (again, the mother is presumed dead). In *The Most Precious Thing in Life* (1934) Jean Arthur plays a woman who never reveals to her son, played by Richard Cromwell, that she is his real mother. One of the more effective and well-known maternal melodramas is *Stella Dallas* (1937). Stella (Barbara Stanwyck) comes from the white underclass and lives in a poor white mill town. She "marries up" to a better class when she weds Stephen (John Boles), a wealthy playboy who was forced to work when his millionaire father, suddenly bankrupt, committed suicide. The couple have a daughter, Laurel (Anne Shirley), but Stephen and Stella are incompatible. Stanwyck's character is marked by behavior that is associated with the white working classes: she is loud, boisterous, and fun. Her husband, after observing the manner in which their white socialite friends obviously find Stella lacking in class, eventually gives up on their relationship. The vicious behavior of the upper-class white women codes them as bad, rich whites. Stella is good-hearted, but she performs her classed whiteness poorly. Ultimately, Stella gives up her daughter so that Laurel doesn't have to be embarrassed by her. In a supreme act of white self-sacrifice, Stella arranges a marriage for her ex-husband with a proper upper-class woman, Helen Morrison

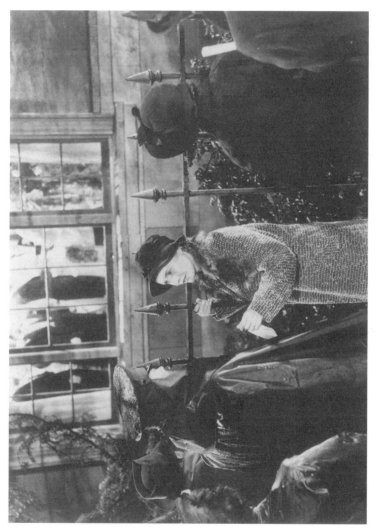

FIGURE 19. Stella Dallas (Barbara Stanwyck) watches from the street as her daughter marries into the upper class in *Stella Dallas* (1937). Courtesy Jerry Ohlinger Archives.

(Barbara O'Neil). "Everyone would naturally think she was your little girl. You're the kind of woman that any girl would be proud of," Stella says. When the child still shows an interest in her own mother, Stella goes further to sacrifice herself: she turns up looking like a drunken prostitute and pretends to marry a drunkard. The end of the movie is almost too much to take, with Stanwyck watching from afar as Laurel is married into the white upper class. The camera cuts to Stanwyck's triumphant yet tear-soaked face. Her sacrifice makes her the ultimate good-white mother; she has reproduced well and has managed to thrust her daughter into upper-class whiteness.

In the little-known but brilliant maternal melodrama *The House on 56th Street* (1933), Kay Francis plays a card shark who becomes a respectable white matron by marriage and class, passing into the world of polite society. She has a child, but a low-down bad-white-male figure from her past returns and tries to rape her. They struggle with a gun, and he ends up dead. Francis is seen standing over him with the gun. Rather than ruin her daughter's life, she goes to prison and lets her child believe she is dead. Years later, released from prison, she sails for Europe. Onboard she meets yet another bad-white male, played by Ricardo Cortez. The two become a team of con artists and are offered a job in a gambling house in New York. To her amazement, the gambling house is the house on Fifty-Sixth Street where she had lived her dream life of married class-passing before her incarceration. Soon mother rescues daughter, a compulsive gambler (played by Margaret Lindsay), but Francis has to kill Cortez's character to save her daughter's dignity. The crime bosses agree to hush up the murder in return for Francis's services in the gambling house. As the film ends, Francis is little more than an indentured servant in the house on Fifty-Sixth Street. White motherhood is the trap in this film.

The white woman in the maternal melodrama is subject to the Victorian white moral code, the vestigial "cult of true womanhood," a code that is impossible to live up to, one that calls for piety, purity, domesticity, and sacrifice. Class-passing through marriage or other plot contrivances is often punished, as is sexuality and the inability to correctly perform white motherhood. Single white mothers or women who have children out of wedlock are always made to suffer. Single white motherhood and single black motherhood are seemingly on trial in the public court of white popular culture today. Eyebrows are raised at single white women, such as Rosie O'Donnell and a host of other white celebrity moms, who choose to adopt. But because of the celebrities' affluence, the public assumes that these adopted children, some born out of wedlock, will not suffer in terms of class. Poor women, regardless of race, who raise children alone are coded as bad mothers in our society. Name a social problem—drugs, gang-related crime, attention deficit disorder, poor academic test scores—and it is often linked (with scanty evidence) to single motherhood. This poorly supported assumption is not only an insult to successful single mothers and successful children of single parents but is another example of how hegemonic whiteness demands compulsory heterosexuality and fosters the myth of the necessity of the perfect nuclear family. To perform whiteness well is to perform heterosexual marriage and parenthood well. The attack is ostensibly on "welfare mothers" of varying ethnicities, but in actuality a predominately white group has been waging a war in Congress and in the media that has portrayed single mothers on welfare as "white trash" or as "crack-addicted," black, lazy societal parasites. Much of the federal money that once supported single mothers has been cut off, and the Welfare Reform Act of 1996 forced single mothers into working, with little regard for child care. White society, it would seem, would rather have a father present in the family, even if he is uninterested in fatherhood, abusive, unemployed, or jailed. White America must not allow women to raise children alone without sanction: single motherhood is a direct threat to patriarchy, heterosexuality, and, perhaps most obliquely, *whiteness itself.* The predominate model of goodness, especially on television, is the white nuclear family. Roseanne Conner of the *Roseanne* show may have been poor white trash, and her husband may sometimes have been out of work, but the family stayed together through thick and thin. *Family Matters, The Cosby Show, The Simpsons, Everybody Loves Raymond,* and *Dharma & Greg* are but a few of the television sitcoms that deny the unraveling of the nuclear family. Single women are often portrayed as disruptive and selfish. The character Ally McBeal (Calista Flockhart) in the eponymous television series started out as a smart, feminist, single white lawyer. She was rapidly transformed, presumably as a result of audience testing, into a stupid, vapid, selfish, mentally imbalanced, generally clueless woman who practices little law and remains helpless in the area of finding the right man. Cybill Shepherd, who played a smart, feminist, successful, white single mother on her series *Cybill,* which lasted only a few seasons before being cancelled, was apparently not the vision of motherhood America wished to embrace. Even *Sabrina, the Teenage Witch,* with two man-hungry witch aunts, is apparently more acceptable; Sabrina does most of her own mothering anyway, so perhaps this series is yet another slap against single motherhood.

Bad-white women abound in Hollywood, from *Leave Her to Heaven* (1945) to *Dark Mirror* (1946) to *Basic Instinct* (1992) to *Fatal Attraction* (1987). Sexual white women are monsters of evil; suffering moms are good, even if they have to do bad things to be sacrificially good. Angela Lansbury starred in *The Manchurian Candidate* (1962) as a double agent who turns her son, played by Laurence Harvey, into a robotic assassin through psychological manipulation. Vicious, bad-white women in film noir include Ann Savage, Claire Trevor, Lana Turner, and Gloria Grahame. More recently, Sharon Stone, Joan Collins, Anjelica Huston, Linda Fiorentino, and Lara Flynn Boyle have performed as vicious, bad-white women. Bad moms and femmes fatales are really not all that different. Femmes fatales refuse to mother their men; instead, they seek to destroy them. Anjelica Huston plays both a bad-white mom and a white femme fatale in *The Grifters* (1990), in which her character seeks to destroy her own son, played by John Cusack. Clay Gregory (Bill Pullman) is up against the vicious Bridget Gregory/Wendy Kroy (Linda Fiorentino) in *The Last Seduction* (1994).

Audiences tiring of narrative films have turned to reality television programs that feature multiple representations of bad whiteness, from cheating romantic partners on *Temptation Island* to vicious and predatory "contestants" on *Survivor,* the first season of which was won by a singularly selfish, uncaring man named Richard Hatch, now a demicelebrity in his own right. *The Weakest Link* is presided over by a black-clad Anne Robinson, who plays the part of host as if she were a cruel British nanny, relentlessly firing questions at contestants who in turn perform against the rules of common decency by voting off other members of the group. One is expected to vote off the poorer players, which always occurred in the original British version. In the American version, however, Robinson is visibly shocked when Americans routinely vote off the brightest people, so that they do not have to compete with someone of equal or superior intelligence in the final rounds. She chastises players who vote off brighter players. *That's not very white of you,* she implies by making them aware of the rules of good (white) sportsmanship. "Is that what they taught you to do in the military?" she asks of one military officer. "It's a dog-eat-dog world," he replies.

Interestingly, Tina Wesson, the winner of the second season of *Survivor*, won by playing the good, motherly nurse figure. She's now a spokesperson for the Arthritis Foundation because she suffers from rheumatoid arthritis. Wesson is portrayed in the media as the good-white woman who won the event because of her sweetness and motherliness. In an article in *Prevention,* where Wesson graced the front cover, the authors portray her as the archetypal good-white woman: "With her Earth Mother disposition and *Steel Magnolias* drawl, Tina was popular with her teammates" (Kiser and Foley 35). Wesson is both mother and sufferer in the archetypal terms used to describe her. The allusion to *Steel Magnolias* (1989) is interesting because *Steel Magnolias* is a maternal melodrama in which the nauseatingly long-suffering Shelby Eatenton Latcherie (Julia Roberts) chooses to give birth to a baby even though the birth will ultimately cause her death. The implication that Tina Wesson is similarly coded as a performing good-white mother is intriguing. Colby Donaldson, the young man who pretty much handed Wesson the victory by not voting her off the island, was clearly behaving as the good-white son. His noble gesture has been scrutinized by the media, as if it goes against the grain of being a proper (greedy, selfish) white player of the game.

The definitions of good and bad whiteness are perhaps going through a shift as we enter a "more postmodern" age, an age in which goodness and whiteness are judged according to material wealth and position. The ability to be a good *consumer* is now more important, it seems, than being a good, chivalrous, young, white male or sport. As long as one has plenty of money, one can be a single mom, a gangsta' thug, or an abusive superstar athlete and still be a hero in the white world. Class now has more to do with cash than with birth relations. Yet with the changes in Western culture, there is a deep nostalgia for a white class that had been based on royal birth and marriage. Diana, Princess of Wales, is emblematic of the good-white female of class and nobility. Though her marriage to Prince Charles was a disaster, the media portrays her as the beneficent, long-suffering good-white mother, who seemingly gave up her party-girl ways to make sure that her sons kept their whitened royal stature. Portrayed as a saint, Diana epitomizes the relationship between white motherhood and blondness and lightness, which is itself a marker of saintliness and religious deity. Paradoxically, we celebrate the dominatrix-like nature of strong, assertive white women, such as the host of *The Weakest Link* (a title that reminds us of our Darwinian past while Diana calls us to our lost class system based on noble birth and acts of charity).

Just as Diana made poverty and the dismantling of lethal land mines her causes, Rosie O'Donnell uses her television show and her fabricated role as the "Queen of Nice" to work toward reducing the number of guns in America. O'Donnell is an unthreatening presence who rewrites what a good-white woman might be. She's a single mom, a self-acknowledged lesbian, and makes absolutely no apologies for her choices. She constantly refers to her motherhood and has recently given up her popular talk show to be a full-time mom. She is like a white version of the black mammy figure. She's sexless, overweight, funny, earnest, and has an on-camera performative style that seems friendly and approachable. She's also sassy in the way that the constructed black mammy was sassy. She is above all a mother to all, which was the role of the mammy figure. She presents no sexual threat to white women because she's not "traditionally" attractive, and yet she carefully performs running gags about how she's sexually attracted to Tom Cruise. She's wise and spirited in the manner of Hattie McDaniel's public persona. She even uses similar performative gestures and mannerisms. O'Donnell stares at the camera to milk a laugh in the same way that McDaniel did. O'Donnell throws back her head and breaks into laughter and song in the same way that Ethel Waters did in her mammy roles. Performing the good white, for Rosie O'Donnell, is a postmodern repertoire of parody, nostalgia, kitsch, and pastiche, which are the hallmarks of postmodernism. She belts out Hollywood standards at the drop of a hat, steeps her show in kitsch, does myriad parodies, and even parodies herself. The bad Anne Robinson of *The Weakest Link* also performs a parody of the brutally stern headmaster at a British prep school, or the mean British nanny, all in a postmodern black-leather out-fit. Being clad entirely in black is "cool," makes an antisociety statement, and is also (in performance situations, whether the theater, film, or tele-vision) traditionally linked to being the "bad" white, just as white cloth-ing is racially linked to being supposedly good in classical Hollywood.

Bad-white men are routinely clad in black, especially in Westerns, film noir, and horror. Bad-white maleness is often associated with effem-inacy, as is the case with Ballin Mundson (George Macready), who is obviously in love with Johnny Farrell (Glenn Ford) in *Gilda* (1946) rather than with Gilda (Rita Hayworth), the alluring white female. Raymond

Burr, who was in reality a gay man, invested his "heavy" roles with an air of authority and corpulent menace. In *Rear Window* (1954) Burr's character (physically patterned after David O. Selznick, whom Hitchcock intensely disliked for his micromanagement during filming of *Rebecca* [1940]) murders his wife, tries to get rid of the body, menaces Grace Kelly's character, and finally tries to kill Jimmy Stewart's wheelchair-bound character. The overweight heavies Victor Buono and Laird Cregar used homosexual performativity to inject bad whiteness into their memorable roles. As Edwin Flagg, Buono is a slobbering mama's boy in *What Ever Happened to Baby Jane?* (1962), but he's not really responsible for his sadism, at least within the context of the film's convoluted narrative. His mother, Mrs. Dehlia Flagg (Marjorie Bennett), an overbearing Cockney white woman who dotes on him obsessively, is the supposed cause of Edwin's passive-aggressive character. As Jack the Ripper in *The Lodger* (1944), or as obsessed police detective Ed Cornell in *I Wake Up Screaming* (1941), Cregar's unruly bulk projects both menace and an undeniable sense of melancholy.

In much of cinema, particularly in film noir, badness in men is routinely linked to female influence. Cody Jarrett's obsession for his mother (James Cagney and Margaret Wycherly, respectively) in *White Heat* (1949) is presented as the cause of Jarrett's rampant viciousness, infantilism, and antisocial behavior, ultimately leading to his spectacular flaming death atop an oil-storage tank. As opposed to such hot personalities, the cinema has also given us a memorable gallery of cold, cruel heavies who have made a good living playing sociopathic bad guys, such as Lee Marvin as a trigger-happy punk in *The Big Heat* (1953), Jack Palance as hired gun Jack Wilson in *Shane* (1953), Dennis Hopper as mad bomber Howard Payne in *Speed* (1994) and as the sociopathic Frank Booth in *Blue Velvet* (1986). There are the white sadists, played by, for example, Clifton Webb, Richard Widmark, Lee Van Cleef, Christopher Walken, and Anthony Hopkins, who has made two films playing the cannibalistic madman Hannibal Lecter. Scratch the surface of nearly any of these characters, and chances are the narrative will present an unfit white mother as a root cause.

Bad-white guys threaten white heterocentric society. They rape women; they steal horses; they try to kill good-white men and women, and they generally terrorize good whites. Bad-white guys are dependent on good-white men and good-white women. Bad-white men are routinely associated with blackness and darkness. They are often involved in the realm of the body, whether they be evil white doctors, evil white sorcerers, or evil white ghouls. Bad-white guys are associated with the unknown, the undead, the mysteries of science. Even white serial killers are complicated, often educated, twisted white men.

Hannibal Lecter in *Silence of the Lambs* (1991) and its sequel, *Hannibal* (2001), is a brilliant if repellent figure. His cannibalistic behavior transgresses the ultimate taboo in white European culture. In Eurocentric society eating humans is routinely and unfairly associated with the African other. Fear of cannibalism is exploited in reams of films that feature (supposed) "African headhunters," especially in films of the mid-to-late twentieth century. When whites contact Africans, no matter what "tribe" the on-screen blacks are supposed to represent, it is assumed that they are headhunters. A running gag in the television show *Gilligan's Island* was the threat of "native headhunters."

White fears of cannibalism are often linked to fears of African spirituality, voodoo, and race mixing. *White Zombie* (1932) stars Bela Lugosi as an evil white sorcerer, Legendre, who uses voodoo to lure a white newlywed couple to his Haitian sugar plantation. Oddly enough, *White Zombie* reenacts white colonial plantation horrors; however, the victims are not Haitians but white Europeans. Legendre makes the good-white newlywed Madeleine Short Parker (Madge Bellamy) into a zombie-slave-mistress because he is obsessed with her beauty. Her ineffectual good-white husband, Neil Parker (John Harron), vainly attempts to save her from an assortment of zombie-slaves that Legendre has similarly entranced. When Legendre accidentally falls to his death, Madeleine suddenly comes to and wonders if it has all been a dream. Madge Bellamy's performance of white femininity as Madeleine is completely passive; she plays the submissive victim. She's docile, dressed in white, seemingly a willing slave. Lugosi, as Legendre, performs evil whiteness as sophisticated and European, yet ghoulish. Legendre uses his privilege and class status to secure knowledge of Haitian voodoo and to colonize the "natives" as zombies. Voodoo is coded as an evil black practice. One of the catch lines used to promote the movie captures the racism inherent in the film: "They knew that this was taking place among the blacks but when this fiend practiced it on a white girl—all hell broke loose." One of the performative methods that Lugosi relies on in *White Zombie* is his gaze. The camera often delivers to the viewer a threateningly tight close-up of his eyes, ablaze with lust. Legendre displays a smug smile throughout the film, seemingly in control of all the island's affairs, and he frequently makes threatening gestures with his eyebrows, but it is his eyes that cast the spell. One of the more memorable techniques used in *White Zombie* is the huge superimposition of Lugosi's eyes on the screen as the couple approaches the town in their coach near the beginning of the film. Legendre's eyes are made even more expressive by the use of optical effects, which make it look as if a bright light is emanating from within. Before we have even met the evil white figure, we have been presented with the vehicle he uses for mastery, his vision.

The gaze of the bad white is routinely associated with mastery over others. In *Dracula* (1931) Count Dracula (Bela Lugosi) uses the power of his gaze to control the men and women whom he chooses as prey or, in the case of Renfield (Dwight Frye), his assistants. A later incarnation of Dracula (Christopher Lee) has power over others through the use of his gaze in *The Horror of Dracula* (1958). The eyes of evil whites have power because vision has been traditionally used in colonialist white culture to control bodies. Many evil white doctors, as routinely portrayed by Boris Karloff, Lionel Atwill, George Zucco, and Colin Clive, are imbued with a gaze that is almost medical. The gaze is associated with the panopticon and is employed in the cinema in a style that visually suggests performing surgery both in gazing at the audience and in involving the audience in subjective gazes of the victims and the perpetrators. Cinema even borrows many terms from medicine.

> A system of "cuts" and "sutures," the cinema borrows much of its technical vocabulary from the discourses of surgical medicine and pathology. The "cut-in," the "cut-away," the "splice," "dissecting editing"—all suggest the capabilities of filmmakers to investigate the human body with the same kind of accuracy, precision, and close scrutiny that pathologists call upon to perform human autopsies. (Fuss 90)

The trope of the destructive, sexually controlling, white, male gaze is often a medical gaze. The camera itself is, after all, capable of seeing things that the human eye cannot; the camera's eye is performative.

As noted, Bela Lugosi's eyes, above all, are the major performative tools on display in *White Zombie*. When his eyes are superimposed on his victim, Madeleine screams, "It felt like hands clutching me." The hypnotic effect of evil eyes is a common trope in the cinema, so popular that it has almost become a parody of itself. The repetitive use of this trope and its parodic variants leads to its subsequent iconic standardization. "Acts become sedimented precisely through the orbit of their historical repetition and desedimented through, shall we say, 'exorbitant' variations on such repetitions, variations that nonetheless also involve repetition, citation, rehearsal, and parody" (McKenzie 223). The evil hypnotic eye is another form of the bad-white body part, but unlike brains, arms, and other limbs that are out of control, the eye connotes mastery.

Voodoo has been replaced by futuristic, all-seeing machines, as in *2001: A Space Odyssey* (1968) and *Alien* (1979). It is interesting to note that the evil robot in *Alien,* Science Officer Ash (Ian Holm), has a decidedly British accent; we do not know that Ash is an android until he goes berserk and attempts to rape Ripley (Sigourney Weaver) more than an hour into the film's running time. Evil in American films is often associated with colonialism, which is in turn associated with the British. The famous voice of HAL, the malevolent computer in *2001: A Space Odyssey,* provided by Douglas Rain, is suffused with a distinctively effeminate sounding attitude that many critics have commented upon. HAL has effectively colonized the ship and killed all the astronauts aboard, and at last he turns his attentions to Dr. David Bowman (Keir Dullea), the last man alive. Bowman forces his way back into the immaculate white precincts of the spaceship and eventually disables HAL but at a considerable cost in human lives. HAL's form of mastery is an ability to see everything on the ship; thus omnipresent visual surveillance is again a metaphor for mastery. Sigourney Weaver, the "final good woman" of *Alien,* has to trick the all-seeing omnipresent Alien in order to destroy it and escape. In *The Matrix* (1999) visuality is an illusion, as the good-white hero, Neo (Keanu Reeves), learns. Reeves plays a computer hacker who lives in a universe controlled by computers. Ultimately, his physical and mental abilities as a white human male help him win his battle, but he is also helped by Morpheus (Laurence Fishburne), an African American who helps him achieve his destiny: saving humanity. It is often the white male's job to save humanity, just as evil white men are often obsessed with destroying the earth. What tasks would James Bond have to accomplish without Ernst Blofeld, Auric Goldfinger, Dr. No, and his other antagonists to contend with? The heroic white male has seemingly godlike duties but is also readily compromised by his all-too-human body and desires.

But white masters need servants and companions; fortunately, the cyborgian future promises to provide both. Dimitra Kessenides found in an interview with robot engineer Stephan Gorevan that it is not so much intelligence as subservience that is being developed in robots.

> Give us forty years, and we'll have a window-washer robot. The ultimate to me is servants in your home. But that servant in your home, you're not going to have a relationship with it. It's going to be like your VCR: when it finally goes, you're not going to be crying. People who say it is going to form an emotional attachment aren't living in the world where money talks. (17)

Whites seem instinctively to want servants, as was demonstrated in all of the classic mainstream films of the 1930s and 1940s and in the *Terminator* series. In the first film, *The Terminator* (1984), Arnold Schwarzenegger plays a violent cyborg that cannot be stopped, but in *Terminator 2: Judgment Day* (1991), which was even more popular, Schwarzenegger returns as the savior of humanity who battles a vicious white cyborg, T-1000, played by Robert Patrick. T-1000 is capable of morphing into any identity—from motorcycle cop to hunk to protoplasmic liquid—and is thus the perfect construct of white villainy. The special effects are really the star of *Terminator 2: Judgment Day,* and the fight between Schwarzenegger and Patrick is easily outdone by the macho heroics of the hyperbuilt Sarah Connor (Linda Hamilton). Increasingly, white heroes are outfitted with superhuman bodies, even partially mechanized parts and android-like features. Perhaps because of its mechanical, dystopian intensity, the *Terminator* series remains popular with audiences, and Schwarzenegger is poised to repeat his role in *Terminator 3* (scheduled for release in late 2002).

Performing whiteness is moving into the realm of performing the body as a cyborg white machine. With the superpowers given to the heroines of *Crouching Tiger, Hidden Dragon* (2000), Hollywood upped the ante both for what is expected in action vehicles and for what is expected of the performative body. *Gladiator* (2000) doesn't so much star goodwhite Maximus Decimus Meridius (Russell Crowe) and bad-white Commodus (Joaquin Phoenix) as it foregrounds the violent special effects. Bodies are hacked to pieces; decapitations and mutilations abound; all of this, of course, is presented (as it was in gladiatorial contests) in the name of public entertainment. Nevertheless, Maximus is suffused with loyalty, strength, and mental acumen, while Commodus is slightly effeminate, has a mother fixation, and is ultimately not quite as bright as the hero.

Gladiator rewrites colonial Roman power struggles through a twentieth-century gaze, as does *The Mummy Returns*. In *The Mummy Returns*, however, the bad figures are ethnic types, nonwhite, larger than life, able to use powers of sorcery, and have the power of the evil gaze. But in most films nonwhites are often simply absent. The absence of African Americans is connected to colonization. As Mary Ann Doane observes,

> The black woman disappears as an actor because she can only be an embarrassment to any lingering ideals of white male morality or white female compassion. . . . The transgressiveness of the notion of the black man "looking back," actively appropriating the gaze, is underlined by its resistance to the biblical myth used to rationalize slavery and colonization. (222–23)

In *Star Wars* (1977) the eerily disembodied voice of James Earl Jones, an African American, was used as the voice of Darth Vader, the ultimate evil force bent on the destruction of the universe. The good-white hero, Luke Skywalker (Mark Hamill), tries to save the world and protect the good-white Princess Leia (Carrie Fisher). Both figures have extraordinary powers and are surrounded by robots, many of which are voiced by African Americans. Darth Vader's uniform is solid black, although his many minions are played by men in futuristic white suits; it is as if George Lucas imagines the evil darkness of Darth Vader as a malign influence on the construct of whiteness. This strategy is carried through in the other films in the series as well, especially in *Star Wars: Episode I— The Phantom Menace* (1999), the most recent episode. Most embarrassing, perhaps, is the figure of Jar Jar Binks (Ahmed Best), who stumbles through the film in a manner reminiscent of Willie Best and Mantan Moreland in their most racist films of the 1940s, all the better to protect the cute white kid of the piece, Anakin Skywalker (Jake Lloyd). *Star Wars* fans so dislike the Jar Jar character, "a rabbit-eared ambulatory lizard whose pidgin English oscillates between crypto-Caribbean patois and Teletubby gurgle" (according to Jim Hoberman ["I Ought"]), that they have anonymously edited and posted a reedited version of the film, available on the Internet, from which Jar Jar has been almost entirely cut. Hoberman amusingly dubs it "The Phantom Edit" (13–14). Whether the fans objected to the character because he was so obviously racist in nature or whether they simply hate him for other reasons is unclear. The brief appearance by Samuel L. Jackson as a black Jedi knight seen sitting in council does little to detract from the white fantasy projection the film represents: the young white boy hero as savior and possible nemesis of the universe.

Yet much of popular commercial fiction remains fixated on the idea of young white male heroes. This is especially true of children's books, many of them created by one Edward Stratemeyer, who founded the Stratemeyer Literary Syndicate and, aided by an army of ghostwriters, created some of the most popular adolescent boy heroes of all time. As David D. Kirkpatrick comments, Stratemeyer's most successful creation was undoubtedly the Hardy Boys series, still being published in updated versions some seventy-five years after their initial appearance in the marketplace.

> The Hardy Boys were first conceived by Edward Stratemeyer, a prolific hack with a nose for business who became the Henry Ford of children's fiction. Mr. Stratemeyer founded a literary syndicate, to mass-produce children's books. He farmed out outlines for formulaic adventures to freelance ghostwriters, and introduced an army of fictional heroes, including Tom Swift, the Bobbsy Twins, Bomba the Jungle Boy and the Hardys' counterpart, Nancy Drew. He created pseudonyms as ostensible authors and kept his writers anonymous, to secure his exclusive control of the franchise. (13)

All of the Hardy Boys books were credited to one "Franklin W. Dixon," but the first and arguably most influential books in the series were written by Leslie McFarlane, a newspaper writer who hammered out such early titles as *The Tower Treasure,* based on Stratemeyer's outline. Other than a brief plot summary, Stratemeyer left the actual writing of the books to his pseudonymous (and anonymous) authors, with a few simple caveats: "[E]ach chapter had to end with a cliffhanger, and no murder, guns, or sex" (Kirkpatrick 13). But at that time, ethnic stereotyping was perfectly acceptable to white readers. Primarily, the series centers on the adventures of two squeaky-clean Hardy Boys, Frank and Joe, two white young men who live in the mythic town of Bayport with their sympathetic father. For a small town, Bayport experiences more than its share of crime, and the Hardy Boys invariably become involved in each new mystery as it unfolds for the reader. But other than the central characters and their associates, the world the Hardy Boys inhabited in their first books was a segregationist's dream.

Nonwhites in the early volumes of the series were used primarily for "humor," as McFarlane elaborated in an interview in his later years. "Negroes were always cowardly, shiftless, lazy and unlettered; Irishmen were incredibly dumb; Jews were avaricious; Scots were stingy; farmers—otherwise known as hayseeds—were credulous idiots" (qtd. in Kirkpatrick 13). Thus the world inhabited by the Hardy Boys in these books is utterly racist, and this is the vision of American society that Stratemeyer and his associates offered to their readers. The series began in the late 1920s, and it was not until 1959 that thirty-eight volumes in the series were revised, in an effort "to rid the texts of ethnic slurs, speed up plots to the pace of the new television world and remove dated references [within the text]" (Kirkpatrick 13). The effort was to some degree successful, and in 1984, Simon & Schuster bought the Stratemeyer syndicate and launched its own update of the series, still written by an invisible army of hired hands. Recent adventures of the Hardy Boys have toyed with Soviet spies, murder, guns, and rock concerts, along with a veritable arsenal of contemporary gadgetry, such as cell phones, computers, and "torn-from-the-headlines adventures involving citywide surveillance systems, corporate whistleblowers, extreme sports and on-line crime" (Kirkpatrick 1). And the updating process seems to be working—the Hardy Boys books still sell more than a million copies annually (1). But what about the lasting impact inculcated by the racism of the first books in the series? For nearly half a century, the books remained repositories of racial prejudice, classified as "children's literature," available to anyone with a library card or a few dollars for a cheap hardcover or paperback edition. How much damage have the Hardy Boys, in their original incarnation, done to the young men growing up in the 1930s to the 1950s who read them? The popularity and influence of the books is undeniable; even today, stripped of its racist stereotypes, the series prospers. Yet has all that much really changed? The Hardy Boys are still white and operate in a nearly all-white fictive universe, with only token attempts at representation of blacks, Latinos, and other marginalized ethnic groups. The domain of whiteness is still the operative social discourse of the city of Bayport, and the Hardy Boys, like the other heroes and heroines of Stratemeyer's series, are still resolutely marked as white.

Like James Gandolfini's Tony Soprano, the likable Mafioso who only wants to keep his family unit together by running drugs, pimping, robbing, and strong-arming his foes, and like President Bill Clinton, who sought to project an image of invincibility even as his lies and infidelities undermined a significant opportunity for social change in American politics, white fictional narratives create a world where white makes right, and people of color exist only as servants or ambiguous token figures, to be called upon or dispensed with at will.

CHAPTER SEVEN

PERFORMING WHITE OTHERNESS

Between the binaries of the white good guys and bad guys and white good women and bad women exists the white other—the ethnic type, the whore, the slattern, the corpse, the fall guy, the victim, the queer, the white trash, the homeless, and the disabled. What of the white human wreckage that skirts the edges of the falsely constructed visual fantasies of whiteness? White others are commonly treated as if they are not fully white. Indeed, it is cinematically "impossible for them to participate in the dominant societal structure, even if they were not already denied admittance on the grounds of their physical unsuitability alone" (Dixon 201).

If we look at traditional (read *white*) cinema from a postmodern perspective, to begin the Lyotardian breakup of the grand narratives, we must first acknowledge their existence and hegemonic power. As I've written elsewhere, we are captive audiences unless we make agency our aim. Onscreen othering prevails and sells as long as we do not question the grand narratives. Hollywood is a plantocracy of images. The extreme racism of jungle films was coproduced by willing audiences.

> Like package tours, audiences desired above all the familiar: to travel to exotic places which are virtually all the same, because you never get to leave the resort hotel once you get to the jungle. At a resort hotel one doesn't interact with the "natives." Instead, the "natives" stage constructed narratives of (supposedly) indigenous customs that have been coproduced by the plantocratic imagination. (*Captive* 71)

The cinematic apparatus is a machine of capture, and "societies are defined by apparatuses of capture" (Deleuze and Guattari 434). By no means does the cinema attempt to capture reality; instead, it captures distorted white hegemonies that are nothing more than clever fictions. Trinh T. Minh-ha writes that, "since fictional and factual have come to a point where they mutually exclude each other, fiction, not infrequently, means lies" (*Woman* 120). One of the greatest lies of the cinema is that the world is largely made up of attractive white people who perform heroic acts and reproduce. It takes a tremendous amount of effort to maintain the lie of whiteness, yet every time an ethnic type is actually portrayed, Hollywood and its audiences congratulate themselves, as if they are themselves breaking up the grand narrative lies of the past. Instead, they are usually heaping on more lies. Ella Shohat dubbed the essential falsity of the mark of the plural, "wherein various ethnic communities and nations are subject to homogenization" (227). The mark of the plural lumps together ethnicities, white or otherwise, as "other" impurities to be cleansed in order to construct whiteness. Furthermore, ethnicities are interchangeable. Jeff Chandler, a Brooklyn Jew born Ira Grossel, made his big breakthrough starring as Cochise in *Broken Arrow* (1950). He was frequently asked to play Native Americans but, oddly, never played a Jew. Jack Palance also successfully played Native Americans. Born Walter Jack Palahnuik, Palance suffered serious facial burns in World War II; as a result, his features were angular, relegating him to roles as heavies and ethnic minorities. In *Arrowhead* (1953), Toriano (Palance) is up against Ed Bannon (Charlton Heston), a cavalry scout who hates Indians, even though he was raised by Apaches. Toriano underestimates Bannon's hatred and treachery, much to his regret. Burt Lancaster and Victor Mature also played Indians, but they were equally at home as Arabs, Egyptians, and even whites. In these images Native Americans are othered as savage, uneducated, and otherwise unspeakable. The master narrative of westerns is that all Indians must be destroyed, even the best of them—the noble savages. Westerns offered whiteness an opportunity to demonstrate its supposed supremacy through their restrictive binary notions of good and bad. The spectacle of the male white body in westerns allowed a space for nostalgia for what never was, the good-white "settler," the civilizing, good-white woman, the bonds of community and friendship in whiteness. Westerns disguise and reinvent one of the most ghastly holocausts on record, the near extermination of the so-called Redskins.

That Orientalism pervades films that feature Asian ethnic types has been well treated by Gina Marchetti in *Romance and the "Yellow Peril"* and

FIGURE 20. Jeff Chandler in race drag as a Native American in *Broken Arrow* (1950). Courtesy Jerry Ohlinger Archives.

by Matthew Bernstein and Gaylyn Studlar in *Visions of the East: Orientalism in Film,* but it is important also to consider the Oriental other as an "almost-white" ethnic type. *The Mask of Fu Manchu* (1932) is a perfect example of a master narrative of filmic Orientalism, with colonialist icon Boris Karloff in the title role, and Myrna Loy, in "yellowface," as his daughter, Fah Lo See. In the film Fu Manchu is obsessed with obtaining the sword of Genghis Khan so that he can rule the world (the usual ambition for racially and/or socially marginalized villains). Loy, in the early part of her career, was trapped in the role of the sadistic, cruel, hypersexual Chinese dominatrix, menacing white men and threatening white women, until she was reborn as the Waspy star of the highly successful *Thin Man* series in 1934 (the series lasted until 1947). In *China Gate* (1957) Angie Dickinson wears yellowface as the Eurasian smuggler Lucky Legs, a Madonna/whore figure who spies for the allies and helps the Americans fight the Communists, even though her white husband left her after she bore him a mixed-race child.

Sidney Toler, a Missouri native with no Asian ancestry, played the omniscient detective Charlie Chan in the long-running series of that name. (Others, including Warner Oland, who was born in Sweden, and Roland Winters, a Boston-bred actor, also took turns playing the role.) Toler's attempt at race drag, complete with the stereotypical clipped speech of a supposed nonnative, is appalling; he most often speaks in fortune-cookie dialogue, spouting neo-Confucian sayings. Chan's cleverness is associated with his ethnicity, but he is always essentially asexual, despite his large off-screen family, which is frequently alluded to as a running gag in the plots of the films, and the presence of "Number 1" or "Number 2" son as an assistant. (Oddly, Chan's cinematic sons were invariably played by genuine Asians, most notably Jimmy Chan.) Charlie Chan posed no sexual threat to the freshly scrubbed white hero in the plot of each film. One could argue that redface makeup and yellowface makeup are not just paint but actually part of the performances of actors who play ethnic types.

Performing whiteness often depends on a backdrop of otherness with signs of ethnicity and the mark of the plural. For example, in *Pardon My Sarong* (1942), Abbott and Costello depend on a human backdrop of "menacing tribesmen," Hollywood "natives," headhunters of a tribe known only to Hollywood. In blackface we see Jews, Irish, African Americans, Italians, Latinos—all blended together to represent the jungle. The

FIGURE 21. Myrna Loy and Boris Karloff in race drag in the Orientalist tract *The Mask of Fu Manchu* (1932). Courtesy Jerry Ohlinger Archives.

jokes of the white comedy team depend on the whiteness of their skin and on its proximity to dark skin. Polynesian, Native American, African, and Caribbean clothing, music, and menace are commingled in Hollywood to prop up the running gags of Bud Abbott and Lou Costello, the good whites who have their own binaries (one's dumb, the other's smart; one's flighty, the other's levelheaded). Ethnic types are not just used to add menace and otherness; they are frequently used to inject sexuality into whiteness. For example, Lupe Velez and Carmen Miranda were used in Hollywood productions to provide eye candy and to represent the supposedly untamable sexual appetites that Latinas frequently signify. Jennifer Lopez trades on her Latinness for the success of her music and films. She seems fully cognizant of the stereotypes thrust on Latinas, but by manipulating those stereotypes and by parodying them, she dismantles them in postmodern fashion, it could be argued, and exposes them as lies; as she does so, however, she runs the risk of being unable ever to play a broader range of characters.

Puerto Rican actor Luis Guzmán is the perennial favorite of casting agents looking for Mexicans, Spaniards, Italians, Latinos, Puerto Ricans, or anyone Latin. He performed in *Magnolia* (1999) and *Boogie Nights* (1997) and has been a frequent guest on various television shows, including *NYPD Blue, Walker, Texas Ranger, Law & Order,* and *The Equalizer.* He often plays the sidekick of the white cop and sometimes plays the heavy, but he usually serves whiteness. He can always be counted on by the white guy to take a bullet, get some evidence, show up with a getaway vehicle, or make a wisecrack that brings together the men, despite ethnic differences.

A "more postmodern" look at the Latino male is available on Fox Television's *That '70s Show.* The comedy poses as a throwback and parodies the middle-class behavior of a prototypical midwestern white nuclear family, headed by a gruff father, Red Forman (played by veteran heavy Kurtwood Smith), and the stay-at-home mother, Kitty Forman (played by Debra Jo Rupp). The teens in the show are all white, with the exception of the character Fez, played by Venezuelan-born Wilmer Valderrama, who is often the butt of racist jokes and performs the swagger of the macho Latino male, yet the self-reflexivity of the show allows the actor to parody his own performance. Fez's clothes, mannerisms, accent, and cocky behavior are sent up in a pastiche of bad 1970s television and its Latino stereotypes, so much so that the "official" web site offers the following:

Where is Fez from? . . . What's his last name?

The writers have decided to keep Fez's home country a mystery. *NO ONE* knows his origin. Similarly, we do not know Fez's real name. Apparently, his real name is unpronounceable, so the guys call him Fez, short for "Foreign Exchange Student." (The spelling is poetic license.) *(That '70s Show)*

His presence and treatment often make the audience uncomfortable because of the frequent breaks with the fourth wall. As Judith Mayne points out, "[C]inema functions *both* to legitimize . . . *and* to challenge" (25).

Images of racist white trash often both legitimize and challenge the white-centered status quo. Flipping through the television channels recently, I came upon a film featuring African American actress Pam Grier, apparently trapped in a shack at the mercy of some racist, good ol' white boys. I was pleased, however, to see how Grier extricated herself from the situation: she quietly siphoned some gasoline through a window, fashioned a Molotov cocktail, threw it at her tormentors, and cheerfully burned them alive. Critics argue over whether *white trash* is a classed or a raced category, but I am really more interested in how *white trash* is othered. I think it is a category that is *both* classed and raced as "low, grotesque other."

Whiteness seems to unravel in dystopian films like *Dirty Harry* (1971), *The Deer Hunter* (1978), and other films associated with white trash. White racists are almost always white trash. William Shatner's portrayal of white racist Adam Cramer in Roger Corman's film *The Intruder* (1961) is indicative of audiences' ability to other racism while not owning up to our own white racism. *American History X* (1998) is a more recent example of displacing white racism onto white trash, with Edward Norton, Edward Furlong, and Fairuza Balk playing kids who are "seduced" into white supremacy and violent racist behavior. The film allows a white audience a comfortable space for projecting its own racism on the bodies of a white other. Whites leave the film stunned by the racist behavior of extremists, but this reaction doesn't lead them to challenge their own everyday racism, nor do they challenge their own white privilege.

The first white privilege we should recognize is that almost all films, video games, television, and American folk narratives are centered on white figures. When we say *mainstream cinema,* we mean *white cinema.* There are exceptions, of course, but Hollywood remains as a "white-making" machine. Outside the United States, however, films are allowed to present a more balanced view. An important work that challenges the myth of the great white hero is Bassek Ba Kobhio's film *The "Great White" of Lambaréné* (*Le Grand blanc de Lambaréné* [1994]), which is but one example of an African decolonized gaze at imperialism and whiteness through the use of a black oppositional gaze. Ba Kobhio, who is emerging as one of the most important and influential voices of the new African cinema, was born in Cameroon in 1957 and initially set out to become a writer. Indeed, he became a widely published short story writer and novelist, winning a prestigious prize for the best short story in French in 1976. He subsequently went on to university schooling and received a diploma in sociology, as well as in philosophy. While he was pursuing his studies, Ba Kobhio started to work part-time as an assistant film director and literary critic, and he eventually enrolled in the cinematography department of the Ministry of Information and Culture.

Ba Kobhio's first major cinematic credit was as assistant director on Claire Denis's film *Chocolat* (1987), which also examines the process of colonialist agency. Ba Kobhio directed his first documentary film in 1988 and his first feature film, *Sango Malo,* in 1990. Of his work in *The "Great White" of Lambaréné,* shot on location in Gabon and Cameroon, with postproduction accomplished in France, Ba Kobhio commented, "I wanted to produce a fragmented film, because time initially rules by constraint, by rape (the start of the film corresponds with the omnipotence of the 'Great White Man'), then, as Africa progressively gains the upper hand, African life takes over" (1). As bell hooks notes, "Spaces of agency exist for Black people, wherein we can both interrogate the gaze of the Other but also look back, and at one another, naming what we see. Subordinates in relations to power learn experientially that there is a critical gaze, one that 'looks' to document, one that is oppositional" (*Reel* 199). An oppositional gaze is employed by many black filmmakers of the African diaspora, from Spike Lee to Julie Dash to Ousmane Sembene. Most often it is called upon to resist further colonial images of Africans and African Americans. In *The "Great White" of Lambaréné,* however, the oppositional gaze is employed as a means of problematizing the spectacle of the great white imperialist figure of Albert Schweitzer, and, in a larger sense, the film problematizes received notions of whiteness itself, especially with regard to power relations, African history, and the memory of white supremacy in postcolonial Africa.

In colonial films whiteness has been presented primarily in the stable forms of such figures as the great white hunter, the great white doctor, the great white civilizer, with occasional departures from these formulas and completely inaccurate and self-serving portrayals. In *The "Great White" of Lambaréné*, a postcolonial African film, however, whiteness is perceived and established by the African oppositional gaze and is dismantled of its privilege and its centeredness. Instead of observing the great white man from the position of white, first-world privilege and political rank, the gaze is reversed and the ethnographic spectacle of the film centers on the study of the perception of the "Great White of Lambaréné," Albert Schweitzer.

As Ba Kobhio argues, Africans perceive whites through a series of notions that are perhaps as strongly defined as the notions whites have of Africanness. "Africans perceive whites as being caricatures, theatrical, obsequious, affected, ruled by time in their everyday lives and by death in the future" (1). Ba Kobhio both demonstrates this perception and problematizes it in many ways in *The "Great White" of Lambaréné*. He dismantles the colonialist version of the life of Dr. Albert Schweitzer (played by André Wilms), and tells his story through the eyes and gaze of a young African named Koumba (Alex Descas), who grows up under the care of Schweitzer and is inspired to become a doctor like the Great White himself. Schweitzer is examined, therefore, from the point of view of a youth who grows into political understanding and eventual conflict with the internationally famous humanitarian. The film ends with the two men locked in conflict, their relationship defined by postcolonial realities, and Koumba is left to bury Schweitzer in Lambaréné with honor, as if he had been a chief, as if he had been his father. Tellingly, Schweitzer's wife, Hélène (Marisa Berenson), is almost entirely marginalized by the film's narrative, which treats her as a figure of absence rather than presence throughout the film. In contrast, Schweitzer's and Koumba's actions are foregrounded throughout the work, as Schweitzer fails to comprehend his own unyielding colonial instincts, and Koumba gradually realizes that he must strike out on his own to achieve true cultural independence from the Great White.

Though whiteness is rarely examined in first-world cinema, it takes center stage in this extraordinary film, and it is divested of its imperialist power. As Dyer notes, "The white spirit organizes white flesh and in turn nonwhite flesh and other material matters: it has enterprise. Imperialism is the key historical form in which that process has been realized" (*White* 15). Albert Schweitzer is depicted in *The "Great White" of Lambaréné* as the ultimate figurehead of white supremacy, which masqueraded as "benevolent" and "great" within the colonialist system. Here, we observe the great white imperial man as paternalistic, disrespectful, egotistical, and ultimately blind to his own failure to connect with the very people he claims to love. His failure is tragic. His depiction is not at all one-sided, however. Schweitzer conforms to African perceptions of whiteness: he is sometimes a caricature, theatrical, obsequious, affected, and ruled by time and very much ruled by his own inability to view life through a decolonized gaze, but he is nevertheless portrayed as a human being who is multifaceted and beyond white stereotype.

To some degree, *The "Great White" of Lambaréné* leads us to the conclusion that Albert Schweitzer was unable to define himself and unable to move beyond the boundaries of whiteness and a white imperial mentality. His paternalistic attitude toward his employees, especially Koumba, the young boy who announces his intention to become a doctor, is a critique of whiteness. There is a strong subtext in this film that suggests that Schweitzer's racism made it impossible for him to truly respect cultural difference. For example, Schweitzer's arrogance and paternalism are displayed by his lack of desire to learn the languages of Africa or to learn from African medicine men. In addition, Schweitzer is limited by his white imperialist understanding of sexuality and kinship systems. Early in the film, for example, Schweitzer treats an African woman who has gonorrhea. He lectures her on sexuality: "It's not like food! You can do without." What he completely misses is that he has shown a lack of understanding of her culture; he has disrespectfully asked her to disobey her husband.

At another point in the film, Schweitzer visits a respected griot, or storyteller, out of desperation, seeking the secrets of the *iboga*. Schweitzer's attempt to purchase secrets is summarily refused. The griot explains that he cannot sell Schweitzer information, and besides, the knowledge of the medicine man is owned by the people, and he must have the permission of the chief to share it. Though seemingly in control of his hospital compound, Schweitzer expresses in this scene his own fear of that which he cannot comprehend, of the forces he calls the "darker powers." In a subsequent scene Schweitzer's wife is teased by one of her servants for being afraid of the cries of the forest animals in the night.

"They eat men," the servant teases Hélène, who seems very ill at ease throughout the film, confined by her position as Schweitzer's silent wife, a witness to events that she cannot control or predict.

Schweitzer is not only trapped by his whiteness but defined by it in ways that mean he must continue the upkeep and maintenance of being the Great White Man, which is remarkably demonstrated by the sequences involving Schweitzer playing the organ and trying to drown out the sounds of African drums outside his window. It is both pathetic and telling that Schweitzer literally tries to erase the sound of African culture, either with European music, particularly Bach, or with the sound of his own voice, lecturing on the "greatness" of the Bible. As an interloper who has never bothered to investigate African culture or language while attempting to "civilize" his patients, Schweitzer is a figure of intolerance and tragic self-delusion. In a hilarious and politically charged sequence, Schweitzer is viewed lecturing Africans on the spiritual nature of work. His words are supposedly translated for him, but there is a remarkable difference between his messages and the subsequent translations. Schweitzer explains, "We are not saved by Jesus' sacrifice on the cross. We must follow it with active commitment. Therefore work in any conditions is an act of salvation." The African translator, however, offers a different version of the text: "Fornicator or drunk, you are sure to have a place in heaven if you work." The scene not only points up the fact that Schweitzer is limited by language but highlights the fact that translation itself is limited because of the vast cultural differences between European and African spirituality. Schweitzer's defective vision is circumscribed by his white European Christianity, even as it motivates him to literally work himself to death in an environment he finds utterly alien. Schweitzer's chosen world is lacking both sufficient Western cultural resources to satisfy his own desires and stable financial backing. Thus Schweitzer is doubly cut off from the society to which he seeks to minister.

The critique of whiteness is not limited, however, to or by Schweitzer. Several African figures specifically address the evils of whiteness as they are attached to white colonialism. Mikendi (Gilbert Nguema), who returns from the war to tell stories of racism he and other Africans experienced at the hands of the French, becomes increasingly politically committed to African independence. He becomes a griot to Koumba. "I hate these whites. I hate them," Mikendi shouts. Mikendi advises Koumba to go abroad, attend medical college, and become a doctor. Then Koumba can return and take over the administration of Lambaréné Hospital. "Let no white hand strike us again," Mikendi admonishes him.

Chief Mata (Athanase Ngou-Ossou) also directly challenges white supremacy and Schweitzer's white imperialist mentality. When Chief Mata asks Schweitzer why he came to Africa if he hates blacks, Schweitzer responds, "I came to save the Blacks," but Chief Mata sees through this imperialistic rhetoric. "You want to rule this kingdom alone and make us all your subjects." But perhaps most critical of Schweitzer is Bissa (Magaly Bertly), his African wife, betrothed to him by Chief Mata. Schweitzer refuses her sexual advances, and she asks him if it is because of her skin color. "You give Africans nothing," she says, and he responds, "I do. My life. My work." "Well, perhaps you give, but you don't share." It is Bissa who also points out to Schweitzer that, though he has seen thousands of African patients, he has made no attempt to understand their languages.

Schweitzer, unable to understand the changes in the African people that come with independence, does not attend the festivities to honor independence day. And he is shocked when Koumba returns, trained as a doctor and lawyer, in the official capacity to take over the administration of the hospital. Schweitzer's response to independence is to retreat into his role as the Great White, and he becomes even less tolerant and more paternalistic and abusive toward the Africans. He forms a relationship with the drummer he has been trying to drown out, but he is the teacher, not the student, never bothering to understand what he may have learned from the African people in terms of music, language, spirituality, or culture. Even this relationship is fraught with paternalistic overtones. Schweitzer buys a trumpet for the drummer and gives it to him. Yet at the same time, Schweitzer refers to the man as "the tom-tom maniac." The complexity of this postcolonial relationship is rendered with great understanding of both sides, and it is beautifully orchestrated by the camerawork and design, which places the drummer outside the walls of Schweitzer's colonial outpost, a prison of his own making, in a way, but also a prison of whiteness and colonial privilege.

Schweitzer's response to independence is to retreat into the past and into fervent denial that his status as a great white colonial man is in question. At about this time, Schweitzer is being considered for the Nobel Peace Prize. The arrival of a white journalist, Ingrid Lombard (Élisabeth Bourgine), marks the arrival of postcolonialism in the world of Albert Schweitzer. For the first time, Schweitzer is attacked and criticized for his behavior, but Schweitzer's initial response is to embrace the moment of the journalist's arrival as a site for his rebuilding of himself into the Great White. Though at first he says there will be no photographs, soon Schweitzer is posing in a series of self-revealing postures of nineteenth-century photographic portraiture. Schweitzer's lack of respect for the African people is evident in the scene in which he and the journalist use Africans as human props. Schweitzer and the journalist pose a group of Africans in a boat with Schweitzer "as if returning from a great trip." This scene is a particularly important deconstruction of the politics of ethnographic photography and of the imperialist controlling of images of African people. It is a self-reflexive moment in a film that emerges from a decolonized gaze. To be confronted with the mechanics of the colonizing gaze of the journalist's camera is to jolt the viewer out of the decolonized gaze and into a position of examining the position inherent in the colonized gaze. This is a deeply pivotal moment in the film, for it enacts on the screen the remarks of Trinh T. Minh-ha, who writes that the goal is "not that merely of correcting the images whites have of non-whites, nor of reacting to the colonial territorial mind by simply reversing the situation and setting up an opposition that at best will hold up a mirror to the Master's activities[;] . . . the question is that of tracking down and exposing the voice of power" ("Outside" 144).

The photograph session is followed by a dinner in which the journalist begins a blistering verbal attack of Schweitzer, including criticism of his administrative policies, his activities as a spy for the Germans in World War II, and his brutality toward indigenous people. Schweitzer refuses to answer the journalist's allegations, but his trusted nurse, Berta (Annie-Marie Moulin), speaks for him, stating, "Don't you punish children in your country?" Here, Berta is exposed as a fervent racist, referring to Africans as children. Later in the film, when she has been divested of all authority, she shouts abuse at her former African patients. "Tell this white woman she must respect us now," an African man says in response. The problematizing of Berta and Schweitzer's white missionary status as racist and paternalistic culminates in Koumba's remark that Schweitzer "only wanted to share in our hell in the hope of reaching heaven." The decolonized African will no longer tolerate being called a primitive or a native, nor will he tolerate the white supremacist myth of the great white doctor-missionary, and he deflates that myth and the man with his statement.

Ironically, upon his death, Schweitzer is made a panther prince and given a proper African funeral. The African people are not trapped by the limits of whiteness in the way that Schweitzer has been. The *"Great White" of Lambaréné* demonstrates the Pan-African capacity for moving beyond cultural difference while recognizing it. Schweitzer, on the other hand, is seen as a dying remnant of "empire," trying desperately to retain a phantom authority he never really possessed. Bassek Ba Kobhio's film is thus a study in microcosm of the entire process of the overthrow of the colonial presence within the African continent, and Schweitzer's presence within the colonial system is seen in a new light. Schweitzer, in his refusal to teach medicine to his assistants, in his refusal to learn the language of the people he ostensibly serves, and in his brutal treatment of his patients, whom he often operates on without benefit of anesthesia (see the opening tooth-extraction sequence for a devastating example of this), far from being the bringer of wisdom and spiritual redemption, is the tool of a colonial government that seeks both to enslave and to degrade its unwilling constituents. The hagiographic Schweitzer of Western colonial legend recedes from our collective vision as Bassek Ba Kobhio's far more realistic portrait of the man emerges. In *The "Great White" of Lambaréné* the historical record of colonialist Africa is rewritten by those who suffered under the oppression it imposed.

Peggy McIntosh, writing about white privilege, lists the circumstances that lead her to reflect on the privilege of her own whiteness. As a white person, McIntosh writes,

> I can turn on the television or open to the front page of the paper and see people of my race widely represented. If I want to, I can be pretty sure of finding a publisher for this piece on white privilege. Whether I use cheques, credit cards or cash, I can count on my skin colour not to work against the appearance of financial reliability. I can swear, or dress in second-hand clothes, or not answer letters, without having people attribute these choices to the bad morals, the poverty or the illiteracy of my race. I am never asked to speak for all the people of my racial group. (75)

The politics of class-passing in the white world clearly needs to be more fully addressed. Passing is "associated with community abandonment and self-annihilation," according to Jane Gaines (19). Performing whiteness is a complex yet unrecognized behavior, both on-screen and off. It is subject to the silence that surrounds discussions of race and class. As

Gilles Deleuze notes, "[T]he body is never in the present" (*Cinema 2* 189), and the white body is as liminal as it is concretized. It is impossible to deconstruct the performance of whiteness even as we live surrounded by images of whiteness and otherness. "Whether the other as other can be grasped at all and whether the self is always only a substitute for the other . . . cannot finally be known" (Fuss 3).

Unless we challenge whiteness and class performativity, we maintain them as the unseen hegemonies that exert a considerable degree of influence over us and over our behavior and our fantasies. There is real work to be done. I am reminded of skin preference every time I hear the news. One body is not worth the same as another body. News anchors report that, for example, thirty thousand people die in an earthquake in India. Then they mention that five Americans were among the dead, as if somehow the five Americans are more worthy. When a person is charged with a crime, his or her race is routinely given, as if the two are inherently related—unless the suspect is white and thus left unmarked. Even queer identity is now being marked as white and comfortably middle class within the idealized, all-white casts of *Queer as Folk* and *Will & Grace.* Whites continue to act as if the burden of difference is on the other. Until whites begin the work of making whiteness strange, little change will come in race relations, even as whiteness threatens to become even more clearly marked by class. Such television programs as *The Jerry Springer Show, Sally Jessy Raphaël, Cops,* and *The Montel Williams Show* make others out of the whites that do not perform their whiteness correctly. They make freaks of sexually transgressive figures such as transgendered and S-M couples. They parade white trash as a spectacle to mock. The cameras zoom in on the outrageous clothing; the "bleep" of the censor punctuates the outrageous language; fights break out so routinely that full-time on-set security personnel are necessary. Poor people of ethnicity are frequent performers on these programs. And yet, even in their denial and repression of difference, audiences are perhaps increasingly able to see the cracks and fissures of class, race, and gender. The body of the other cannot be fully contained by the visual.

Whiteness is destabilizing even as we watch. In an interview with Polish immigrant youths, Joel L. Swerdlow found that high school students are increasingly suspicious of the label of whiteness as it is applied in American society.

"I don't want to be white," says a white student from Poland . . . others agree with the Polish born youth, but I'm confused. They explain. To call someone "white" is an insult, as are synonymous terms like Wonder bread. "I don't consider myself white," says a young woman from Russia. She has white skin. "Whites act white and do white stuff . . . white kids act different. They hang out differently. Whites are privileged." . . . [Other students agree, and one notes that] "when you go to apply for a job . . . you have to act white." . . . [For these students], white is not cool. (55)

It remains to be seen if white performativity will be reinscribed in new forms of narrative, such as digital interactive video games. Meanwhile, many are actively challenging white dominance in visual narratives, and these challenges also serve to disrupt the supposed hegemony of whiteness and other cultural norms.

WORKS CITED AND CONSULTED

Abel, Elizabeth. "Black Writing, White Reading: Race and the Politics of Feminist Interpretation." *Critical Inquiry* 19.3 (Spring 1993): 470–98.

Acker, Ally. *Reel Women: Pioneers of the Cinema, 1896 to the Present.* New York: Continuum, 1993.

A.I. Advertisement. *New York Times* 13 May 2001, sec. 2: 7.

Allen, Theodore W. *The Invention of the White Race: The Origin of Racial Oppression in Anglo-America.* London: Verso, 1997.

Aparicio, Frances R., and Susana Chávez-Silverman, eds. *Tropicalizations: Transcultural Representations of "Latinidad."* Hanover, NH: UP of New England, 1997.

Appiah, K. Anthony, and Amy Gutmann. *Color Conscious: The Political Morality of Race.* Princeton: Princeton UP, 1996.

Atkinson, Michael. *Ghosts in the Machine: The Dark Heart of Pop Cinema.* New York: Proscenium, 1999.

Babb, Valerie. *Whiteness Visible: The Meaning of Whiteness in American Literature and Culture.* New York: New York UP, 1998.

Bakhtin, Mikhail. *The Dialogic Imagination.* Trans. Carl Emerson and Michael Holquist. Austin: U of Texas P, 1981.

Ba Kobhio, Bassek. Press release. "Albert Schweitzer: The 'Great White' of Lambaréné." Brooklyn Museum, New York, 1996.

Baldwin, James. "On Being 'White' . . . and Other Lies." *Black on White: Black Writers on What It Means to Be White.* Ed. David R. Roediger. New York: Schocken Books, 1998. 177–80.

Banta, Martha. *Taylored Lives: Narrative Productions in the Age of Taylor, Veblen, and Ford.* Chicago: U of Chicago P, 1993.

Barker, Jennifer M. "Bodily Irruptions: The Corporeal Assault on Ethnographic Narration." *Cinema Journal* 34.3 (1995): 57–76.

Basinger, Jeanine. *A Woman's View: How Hollywood Spoke to Women, 1930–1960.* New York: Knopf, 1993.

Baudrillard, Jean. *Forget Foucault.* Trans. Nicole Dufresne. New York: Semiotext(e), 1987.

———. *The Illusion of the End.* Trans. Chris Turner. Stanford: Stanford UP, 1994.

———. *Seductions.* Trans. Brian Singer. New York: St. Martin's, 1990.

———. *Simulacra and Simulation.* Trans. Sheila Faria Glaser. Ann Arbor: U of Michigan P, 1994.

Bergson, Henri. *Matter and Memory.* Trans. Nancy Margaret Paul and W. Scott Palmer. New York: Zone, 1988.

Bernardi, Daniel. "The Voice of Whiteness: D. W. Griffith's Biograph Films (1908–1913)." Ed. Daniel Bernardi. *The Birth of Whiteness: Race and the Emergence of U.S. Cinema.* New Brunswick: Rutgers UP, 1996. 103–28.

Bernstein, Matthew, and Gaylyn Studlar, eds. Visions of the East: Orientalism in Film. New Brunswick, Rutgers UP, 1997.

Bhabha, Homi K. *The Location of Culture.* London: Routledge, 1994.

Bobo, Jacqueline. *Black Women as Cultural Readers.* New York: Columbia UP, 1995.

Bogle, Donald. *Toms, Coons, Mulattoes, Mammies, and Bucks: An Interpretive History of Blacks in American Film.* New York: Continuum, 1989.

Bowers, Eileen. *The History of American Cinema II: The Transformation of Cinema, 1907–1915.* New York: Scribner's, 1990.

Bowser, Pearl, and Louise Spence. "Identity and Betrayal: *The Symbol of the Unconquered* and Oscar Micheaux's 'Biographical Legend.'" *The Birth of Whiteness: Race and the Emergence of U.S. Cinema.* Ed. Daniel Bernardi. New Brunswick: Rutgers UP, 1996. 56–80.

Brody, Jennifer DeVere. *Impossible Purities: Blackness, Femininity, and Victorian Culture.* Durham, NC: Duke UP, 1998.

Butler, Judith. *Gender Trouble: Feminism and the Subversion of Identity.* New York: Routledge, 1999.

Butterfield, Fox. "Victims' Race Affects Decisions on Killers' Sentence, Study Finds." *New York Times* 20 Apr. 2001: A10.

Cameron, Kenneth M. *Africa on Film: Beyond Black and White.* New York: Continuum, 1994.

Campbell, Edward D. C. *The Celluloid South: Hollywood and the Southern Myth.* Knoxville: U of Tennessee P, 1981.

Canedy, Dana. "Florida Governor Calls Commission Report on Election Biased." *New York Times* 6 June 2001: A20.

Carby, Hazel. *Reconstructing Womanhood.* New York: Oxford UP, 1987.

Cartwright, Lisa. *Screening the Body: Tracing Medicine's Visual Culture.* Minneapolis: U of Minnesota P, 1995.

Castillo, Ana. *Massacre of the Dreamers: Essays on Xicanisma.* New York: Penguin, 1994.

Chaudhuri, Nupur, and Margaret Strobel, eds. *Western Women and Imperialism: Complicity and Resistance.* Bloomington: Indiana UP, 1992.

Ching-Liang Low, Gail. *White Skins/Black Masks: Representation and Colonialism.* London: Routledge, 1996.

Chow, Rey. *Writing Diaspora: Tactics of Intervention in Contemporary Cultural Studies.* Bloomington: Indiana UP, 1993.

Clover, Carol J. *Men, Women, and Chain Saws: Gender in the Modern Horror Film.* Princeton: Princeton UP, 1992.

Cohan, Steven, and Ina Rae Hark, eds. *Screening the Male: Exploring Masculinities in Hollywood Cinema.* London: Routledge, 1993.

Cohen-Cruz, Jan, ed. *Radical Street Performance: An International Anthology.* London: Routledge, 1998.

Cripps, Thomas. *Making Movies Black: The Hollywood Message Movie from World War II to the Civil Rights Era.* New York: Oxford UP, 1993.

———. *Slow Fade to Black: The Negro in American Film, 1900–1942.* New York: Oxford UP, 1977.

Davis, F. James. *Who Is Black? One Nation's Definition.* University Park: Penn State UP, 1993.

Davis, Natalie Zemon. *Slaves on Screen: Film and Historical Vision.* Cambridge: Harvard UP, 2000.

Davis, Tracy C. "The Social Dynamic and 'Respectability.'" Ed. Lizbeth Goodman with Jane de Gay. *The Routledge Reader in Gender and Performance.* London: Routledge, 1998. 70–73.

Debord, Guy. *The Society of the Spectacle.* Trans. Donald Nicholson-Smith. New York: Zone, 1995.

de Certeau, Michel. *The Practice of Everyday Life.* Trans. Steven Rendall. Berkeley: U of California P, 1984.

Deleuze, Gilles. *Cinema 1: The Movement—Image.* Trans. Hugh Tomlinson and Barbara Habberjam. Minneapolis: U of Minnesota P, 1986.

———. *Cinema 2: The Time Image.* Trans. Hugh Tomlinson and Robert Galeta. Minneapolis: U of Minnesota P, 1989.

Deleuze, Gilles, and Félix Guattari. *A Thousand Plateaus: Capitalism and Schizophrenia.* Trans. Brian Massumi. Minneapolis: U of Minnesota P, 1996.

Desowitz, Bill. "New Apes, New Planet, Old Story: Simians Still Rule." *New York Times* 13 May 2001, sec. 2: 3+.

Diawara, Manthia. "Black Spectatorship: Problems of Identification and Resistance." *Black American Cinema.* Ed. Manthia Diawara. New York: Routledge, 1993. 211–20.

———, ed. *Black American Cinema.* New York: Routledge, 1993.

Dixon, Wheeler Winston. "Archetypes of the Heavy in the Classical Hollywood Cinema." *Beyond the Stars: Studies in American Popular Film,* Volume I, *Stock Characters in American Popular Film.* Ed. Paul Loukides and Linda K. Fuller. Bowling Green: Bowling Green State UP, 1990. 201–11.

Doane, Mary Ann. *Femmes Fatales: Feminism, Film Theory, Psychoanalysis.* New York: Routledge, 1991.

Doherty, Thomas. *Pre-Code Hollywood: Sex, Immorality, and the Insurrection in American Cinema, 1930–1934.* New York: Columbia UP, 1999.

Donaldson, Laura E. *Decolonizing Feminism: Race, Gender, and Empire Building.* Chapel Hill: U of North Carolina P, 1992.

Du Bois, W. E. B. "The Souls of White Folk." *Black on White: Black Writers on What It Means to Be White.* Ed. David R. Roediger. New York: Schocken Books, 1998. 184–99.

During, Simon, ed. *The Cultural Studies Reader.* London: Routledge, 1993.

Dyer, Richard. *Stars.* London: BFI, 1998.

————. *White.* London: Routledge, 1997.

————. "White." *Screen* 29.4 (1988): 44–65.

Ellison, Ralph. "What America Would Be without Blacks." *Black on White: Black Writers on What It Means to Be White.* Ed. David R. Roediger. New York: Schocken Books, 1998. 160–71.

Elsaesser, Thomas. "Ethnicity, Authenticity, and Exile: A Counterfeit Trade? German Filmmakers and Hollywood." *Home, Exile, Homeland: Film, Media, and the Politics of Place.* Ed. Hamid Naficy. New York: Routledge, 1999. 97–123.

Erdmann, Robert. "Heath Ledger Is Wise to You, Hollywood." *GQ* June 2001: 168–73.

Everett, Anna. *Returning the Gaze: A Genealogy of Black Film Criticism, 1909–1949.* Durham, NC: Duke UP, 2001.

Fagelson, William Friedman. "Fighting Films: The Everyday Tactics of World War II Soldiers." *Cinema Journal* 40.3 (2001): 94–112.

Fanon, Frantz. *Black Skin, White Masks: The Experiences of a Black Man in a White World.* Trans. Charles Lam Markmann. New York: Grove, 1967.

Felski, Rita. "Nothing to Declare: Identity, Shame, and the Lower Middle Class." *PMLA* 115 (2000): 33–45.

Fine, Michelle, Lois Weiss, Linda C. Powell, L. Mun Wong, eds. *Off White: Readings on Race, Power, and Society.* New York: Routledge, 1997.

Fischer, Lucy. *Shot/Countershot: Film Tradition and Women's Cinema.* Princeton: Princeton UP, 1989.

————. *Written by Herself.* Bloomington: Indiana UP, 1993.

Foster, Gwendolyn Audrey. *Captive Bodies: Postcolonial Subjectivity in Cinema.* Albany: State U of New York P, 1999.

————. "Performativity and Gender in Alice Guy's *La Vie du Christ.*" *Film Criticism* 22.1 (Fall 1998): 6–17.

————. *Troping the Body: Gender, Etiquette, and Performance.* Carbondale: Southern Illinois UP, 2000.

———. *Women Film Directors: An International Bio-Critical Dictionary.* Westport, CT: Greenwood, 1995.

———. *Women Filmmakers of the African and Asian Diaspora: Decolonizing the Gaze, Locating Subjectivity.* Carbondale: Southern Illinois UP, 1997.

Foster, Hal. *The Return of the Real.* Cambridge: Massachusetts Institute of Technology P, 1996.

Foucault, Michel. *Discipline and Punish: The Birth of the Prison.* Trans. Alan Sheridan. New York: Vintage, 1979.

———. *The History of Sexuality.* Trans. Robert Hurley. New York: Pantheon, 1978.

———. *The Order of Things: An Archeology of the Human Sciences.* New York: Vintage, 1973.

Frankenberg, Ruth. *White Women, Race Matters: The Social Construction of Whiteness.* Minneapolis: U of Minnesota P, 1993.

———, ed. *Displacing Whiteness: Essays in Social and Cultural Criticism.* Durham, NC: Duke UP, 1997.

Frederickson, George. *The Comparative Imagination: On the History of Racism, Nationalism, and Social Movements.* Berkeley: U of California P, 1997.

Friedman, Lester D., ed. *Unspeakable Images: Ethnicity and the American Cinema.* Urbana: U of Illinois P, 1991.

Fuss, Diana. *Identification Papers.* New York: Routledge, 1995.

Gaines, Jane. "White Privilege and Looking Relations: Race and Gender in Feminist Film Theory." *Screen* 29.4 (1988): 12–27.

Geuens, Jean-Pierre. *Film Production Theory.* Albany: State U of New York P, 2000.

Gilman, Sander. *Difference and Pathology: Stereotypes of Sexuality, Race, and Madness.* Ithaca: Cornell UP, 1985.

Giroux, Henry A. *Disturbing Pleasures: Learning Popular Culture.* New York: Routledge, 1994.

Glenhill, Christine, ed. *Home Is Where the Heart Is: Studies in Melodrama and the Woman's Film.* London: BFI, 1987.

Goffey, Andy. "Nature = *x:* Notes on Spinozist Ethics." *The Virtual Embodied: Presence/Practice/Technology.* Ed. John Wood. London: Routledge, 1998. 63–75.

Gordon, Lewis. "From *Bad Faith and Antiblack Racism*." *Black on White: Black Writers on What It Means to Be White*. Ed. David R. Roediger. New York: Schocken Books, 1998. 305–6.

Green, Eric. Planet of the Apes *as American Myth: Race and Politics in the Films and the Television Series*. Jefferson, NC: McFarland, 1996.

Gubar, Susan. *Racechanges: White Skin, Black Face in American Culture*. New York: Oxford UP, 1997.

Guerrero, Ed. *Framing Blackness: The African American Image in Film*. Philadelphia: Temple UP, 1993.

Hale, Grace Elizabeth. *Making Whiteness: The Culture of Segregation in the South, 1890–1940*. New York: Schocken Books, 1998.

Haney, Lopez Ian. *White By Law: The Legal Reconstruction of Race*. New York: New York UP, 1996.

Hansen, Miriam. *Babel and Babylon: Spectatorship and American Silent Film*. Cambridge: Harvard UP, 1991.

Haraway, Donna. *Primate Visions: Gender, Race, and Nature in the World of Modern Science*. New York: Routledge, 1989.

Harris, Cheryl. "Whiteness As Property." *Black on White: Black Writers on What It Means to Be White*. Ed. David R. Roediger. New York: Schocken Books, 1998. 103–18.

Harris, Trudier. "White Men as Performers in the Lynching Ritual." *Black on White: Black Writers on What It Means to Be White*. Ed. David R. Roediger. New York: Schocken Books, 1998. 299–304.

Harrison, Daphne Duval. *Black Pearls: Blues Queens of the 1920s*. New Brunswick: Rutgers UP, 1988.

Hart, Lynda, and Peggy Phelan, eds. *Acting Out: Feminist Performances*. Ann Arbor: U of Michigan P, 1991.

Hawkins, Joan. *Cutting Edge: Art-Horror and the Horrific Avant-garde*. Minneapolis: U of Minnesota P, 2000.

Herbert, Bob. "'Lousy List' Keeps Florida Blacks from Voting for President." *International Herald Tribune* 9–10 Dec. 2000: 8.

Hetty Green—The Witch of Wall Street Web Site. 24 Aug. 2001 <http://www.witchofwallstreet.com/main.htm>.

Hill, Mike, ed. *Whiteness: A Critical Reader.* New York: New York UP, 1997.

Hitchcock, Peter. "They Must Be Represented? Problems in Theories of Working-Class Representation." *PMLA* 115 (2000): 20–32.

Hoberman, Jim. "I Ought to Be in Pictures." *New York Times Magazine* 15 July 2001: 13–14.

———. "Work in Progress." *Village Voice* 4 Apr. 2000: 121.

Holmes, Steven A. "The Confusion over Who We Are." *New York Times* 3 June 2001, sec. 4: 1.

hooks, bell. *Black Looks: Race and Representation.* Boston: South End, 1992.

———. *Reel to Real: Race, Sex, and Class at the Movies.* New York: Routledge, 1996.

———. *Where We Stand: Class Matters.* New York: Routledge, 2000.

Hutcheon, Linda. *A Poetics of Postmodernism: History, Theory, Fiction.* New York: Routledge, 1988.

Huxley, Michael, and Noel Witts, eds. *The Twentieth Century Performance Reader.* London: Routledge, 1996.

Hylton, Wil S. "Who Owns This Body?" *Esquire* June 2001: 102+.

Ignatiev, Noel. *How the Irish Became White.* New York: Routledge, 1995.

———, and John Garvey, eds. *Race Traitor.* New York: Routledge, 1996.

Jacobson, Matthew Frye. *Whiteness of a Different Color: European Immigrants and the Alchemy of Race.* Cambridge: Harvard UP, 1998.

Jameson, Fredric. Foreword. *The Postmodern Condition: A Report on Knowledge,* by Jean-François Lyotard. Trans. Geoff Bennington and Brian Massumi. Minneapolis: U of Minnesota P, 1991. vii–xxi.

Jarvie, Ian C. "Stars and Ethnicity: Hollywood and the United States, 1932–51." *Unspeakable Images: Ethnicity and the American Cinema.* Ed. Lester D. Friedman. Urbana: U of Illinois P, 1991. 82–111.

Joseph, May, and Jennifer Natalya Fink, eds. *Performing Hybridity.* Minneapolis: U of Minnesota P, 1999.

Kaplan, E. Ann. *Looking for the Other: Feminism, Film, and the Imperial Gaze.* New York: Routledge, 1997.

Katz, Jonathan Ned. *The Invention of Heterosexuality.* New York: Penguin, 1995.

Kessenides, Dimitra. "Questions for Stephan Gorevan." *New York Times Magazine* 17 June 2001: 17.

Kirkpatrick, David D. "In Latest Hardy Boys Case, a Search for New Readers." *New York Times* 29 July 2000, sec. 1: 1+.

Kiser, Sherry Weiss, and Denise Foley. "Tina Wesson: A True Survivor." *Prevention* Aug. 2001: 34–35.

Klawans, Stuart. "Legionnaire's Disease." *Nation* 17 Apr. 2000: 34–36.

A Knight's Tale. Advertisement. *New York Times* 13 May 2001, sec. 2A: 2.

Kruger, Barbara. *Remote Control: Power, Cultures, and the World of Appearances.* Cambridge: Massachusetts Institute of Technology P, 1993.

Lipsitz, George. *The Possessive Investment in Whiteness: How White People Profit from Identity Politics.* Philadelphia: Temple UP, 1998.

López, Ana M. "Are All Latins from Manhattan? Hollywood, Ethnography, and Cultural Colonialism." *Unspeakable Images: Ethnicity and the American Cinema.* Ed. Lester D. Friedman. Urbana: U of Illinois P, 1991. 404–24.

Lott, Eric. "The Whiteness of Film Noir." *Whiteness: A Critical Reader.* Ed. Mike Hill. New York: New York UP, 1997. 81–101.

Lyotard, Jean-François. *The Postmodern Condition: A Report on Knowledge.* Trans. Geoff Bennington and Brian Massumi. Minneapolis: U of Minnesota P, 1991.

Macintire, Alice. *Making Meaning in Whiteness.* Albany: State U of New York P, 1997.

Manring, M. M. *Slave in a Box: The Strange Career of Aunt Jemima.* Charlottesville: UP of Virginia, 1998.

Marchetti, Gina. *Romance and the "Yellow Peril": Race, Sex, and Discursive Strategies in Hollywood Fiction.* Berkeley: U of California P, 1993.

Marks, Laura U. *The Skin of the Film: Intercultural Cinema, Embodiment, and the Senses.* Durham: Duke UP, 2000.

Martin, Michael T., ed. *Cinemas of the Black Diaspora.* Detroit: Wayne State UP, 1995.

Maynard, Richard A. *Africa on Film: Myth and Reality.* Rochelle Park, NJ: Hayden, 1974.

Mayne, Judith. *The Women at the Keyhole.* Bloomington: Indiana UP, 1990.

McIntosh, Peggy. "White Privilege and Male Privilege: A Personal Account of Coming to See Correspondences through Work in Women's Studies." *Race, Class, and Gender: An Anthology.* Ed. Margaret L. Andersen and Patricia Hill Collins. Belmont, CA: Wadsworth, 1992. 70–81.

McKee, Patricia. *Producing American Races: Henry James, William Faulkner, Toni Morrison.* Durham, NC: Duke UP, 1999.

McKenzie, Jon. "Genre Trouble: (The) Butler Did It." *The Ends of Performance.* Ed. Peggy Phelan and Jill Lane. New York: New York UP, 1998. 217–35.

McMahan, Alison. *Alice Guy Blaché: Cinematic Visionary.* Forthcoming; New York: Continuum, 2002.

———. *A Fool and His Money* Web Site. 14 July 2001 <http://www.mdle.com/ClassicFilms/Guest/mcmahan2.htm>.

Mead, Rebecca. "Eggs for Sale." *New Yorker* 9 Aug. 1999: 56–65.

Melville, Herman. *Billy Budd, Foretopman.* Ed. F. Barron Freeman. Cambridge: Harvard UP, 1948.

Mercer, Kobena. *Welcome to the Jungle: New Positions in Black Cultural Studies.* New York: Routledge, 1994.

Miller, Nancy K. "Representing Others: Gender and the Subjects of Autobiography." *Differences* 6.1 (1994): 1–27.

Mills, Charles W. *The Racial Contract.* Ithaca: Cornell UP, 1997.

Monk, John. "The Digital Unconscious." *The Virtual Embodied: Presence/Practice/Technology.* Ed. John Wood. London: Routledge, 1998. 30–44.

Morley, David, and Kuan-Hsing Chen, eds. *Stuart Hall: Critical Dialogues in Cultural Studies.* London: Routledge, 1996.

Morrison, Toni. *Playing in the Dark: Whiteness and the Literary Imagination.* Cambridge: Harvard UP, 1992.

Morton, Walt. "Tracking the Sign of *Tarzan:* Trans-Media Representations of a Pop-Culture Icon." *You Tarzan: Masculinity, Movies, and Men.* Ed. Pat Kirkham and Janet Thumin. New York: St. Martin's, 1993. 106–25.

Musser, Charles. "Ethnicity, Role-Playing, and American Film Comedy: From *Chinese Laundry Scene* to *Whoopee* (1894–1930)." *Unspeakable Images: Ethnicity and the American Cinema.* Ed. Lester D. Friedman. Urbana: U of Illinois P, 1991. 39–81.

Newitz, Annalee, and Matthew Wray. "What Is 'White Trash'? Stereotypes and Economic Conditions of Poor Whites in the United States." *Whiteness: A Critical Reader.* Ed. Mike Hill. New York: New York UP, 1997. 168–84.

Nichols, Bill. *Blurred Boundaries.* Bloomington: Indiana UP, 1994.

Obeyesekere, Gananath. *The Work of Culture: Symbolic Transformation in Psychoanalysis and Anthropology.* Chicago: U of Chicago P, 1990.

Ong, Aihwa. "Colonialism and Modernity: Feminist Re-Presentations of Women in Non-Western Societies." *Theorizing Feminism: Parallel Trends in the Humanities and Social Sciences.* Ed. Ann C. Herrmann and Abigail Steward. Boulder: Westview, 1994. 372–81.

Penn, W. S., ed. *As We Are Now: Mixblood Essays on Race and Identity.* Berkeley: U of California P, 1997.

Phelan, Peggy. *Unmarked: The Politics of Performance.* London: Routledge, 1993.

———, and Jill Lane, eds. *The Ends of Performance.* New York: New York UP, 1998.

Pieterse, Jan Nederveen. *White on Black: Images of Africa and Blacks in Western Popular Culture.* New Haven: Yale UP, 1992.

Rabinovitz, Lauren. *For the Love of Pleasure: Women, Movies, and Culture in Turn-of-the Century Chicago.* New Brunswick: Rutgers UP, 1998.

Reid, Mark A. "Dialogic Modes of Representing African(s): Womanist Film." *Cinemas of the Black Diaspora.* Ed. Michael T. Martin. Detroit: Wayne State UP, 1995. 56–69.

———. *PostNegritude Visual and Literary Culture.* Albany: State U of New York P, 1997.

———. "Rebirth of a Nation: Three Recent Films Resist Southern Stereotypes of D. W. Griffith, Depicting a Technicolor Region of Black, Brown, and Gray." *Southern Exposure* 20.4 (1992): 26–28.

Rodriguez, Gregory. "Who Are You? When Perception Is Reality." *New York Times* 3 June 2001, sec. 4: 1+.

Rogin, Michael. *Blackface, White Noise: Jewish Immigrants in the Hollywood Melting Pot.* Berkeley: U of California P, 1996.

Rony, Fatimah Tobing. *The Third Eye: Race, Cinema, and Ethnographic Spectacle.* Durham, NC: Duke UP, 1996.

Rowe, Kathleen. *The Unruly Woman: Gender and the Genres of Laughter.* Austin: U of Texas P, 1995.

Russo, Vito. *The Celluloid Closet.* New York: Harper, 1985.

Said, Edward W. *Culture and Imperialism.* New York: Knopf, 1993.

————. *Representations of the Intellectual.* New York: Vintage, 1994.

Saldivar, José. *Border Matters: Remapping American Cultural Studies.* Berkeley: U of California P, 1997.

Saulny, Susan. "And There Was Light, and It Was Good?" *New York Times* 2 Sept. 2001, sec. 4: 3.

Schiebinger, Londa. *Nature's Body: Gender in the Making of Modern Science.* Boston: Beacon, 1993.

Schocket, Eric. "'Discovering Some New Race': Rebecca Harding Davis's 'Life in the Iron Mills' and the Literary Emergence of Working-Class Whiteness." *PMLA* 115 (2000) 46–59.

Seltzer, Mark. *Bodies and Machines.* New York: Routledge, 1992.

Seshadri-Crooks, Kalpana. *Desiring Whiteness: A Lacanian Analysis of Race.* London: Routledge, 2000.

Sharpe, Jenny. "Figures of Colonial Resistance." *The Post-Colonial Studies Reader.* Ed. Bill Ashcroft, Gareth Griffiths, and Helen Tiffin. London: Routledge, 1995. 99–103.

Shaviro, Steven. *The Cinematic Body.* Minneapolis: U of Minnesota P, 1993.

Shohat, Ella. "Ethnicities-in-Relation: Toward a Multicultural Reading of American Cinema." *Unspeakable Images: Ethnicity and the American Cinema.* Ed. Lester D. Friedman. Urbana: U of Illinois P, 1991. 216–50.

Slemon, Stephen. "Unsettling the Empire: Resistance Theory for the Second World." *The Post-Colonial Studies Reader.* Ed. Bill Ashcroft, Gareth Griffiths, and Helen Tiffin. London: Routledge, 1995. 104–10.

Smith, Valerie. *Not Just Race, Not Just Gender: Black Feminist Readings.* New York: Routledge, 1998.

Smith-Rosenberg, Carroll. *Disorderly Conduct: Visions of Gender in Victorian America.* New York: Oxford UP, 1985.

Snead, James. *White Screens/Black Images: Hollywood from the Dark Side.* New York: Routledge, 1994.

Sobchack, Vivian. *The Address of the Eye: A Phenomenology of Film Experience.* Princeton: Princeton UP, 1992.

———. *Screening Space: The American Science Fiction Film.* New York: Ungar, 1987.

Somerville, Siobhan B. *Queering the Color Line: Race and the Invention of Homosexuality in American Culture.* Durham: Duke UP, 2000.

Spivak, Gayatri. "Can the Subaltern Speak?" *Marxism and the Interpretation of Culture.* Ed. Cary Nelson and Lawrence Grosberg. Urbana: U of Illinois P, 1988. 271–316.

Stacey, Jackie. *Star Gazing: Hollywood Cinema and Female Spectatorship.* London: Routledge, 1994.

Staiger, Janet. *Bad Women: Regulating Sexuality in Early American Cinema.* Minneapolis: U of Minnesota P, 1995.

Stamp, Shelley. *Movie-Struck Girls: Women and Motion Picture Culture after the Nickelodeon.* Princeton: Princeton UP, 2000.

Stokes, Mason. *The Color of Sex: Whiteness, Heterosexuality, and the Fictions of White Supremacy.* Durham, NC: Duke UP, 2001.

Swerdlow, Joel L. "Changing America." *National Geographic* Sept. 2001: 42+.

Taubin, Amy. "Claire Denis's Band of Outsiders." *Village Voice* 4 Apr. 2000: 126.

That '70s Show Web Site. 9 Sept. 2001 <http://www.that70sshow.com/index_faq.htm>.

Trinh T. Minh-ha. *Framer Framed.* New York: Routledge, 1992.

———. "Outside In, Inside Out." *Questions of Third Cinema.* Ed. Jim Pines and Paul Williams. London: BFI, 1989. 133–49.

———. *Woman, Native, Other: Writing, Postcoloniality, and Feminism.* Bloomington: Indiana UP, 1989.

Veblen, Thorstein. *The Theory of the Leisure Class.* London: Dover, 1994.

Vincentelli, Elisabeth. "Agnès Godard's Candid Camera." *Village Voice* 11 Apr. 2000: 166.

Vron, Ware. *Beyond the Pale: White Women, Racism, and History.* London: Verso, 1992.

Wade, Nicholas. "Genome Mappers Navigate the Tricky Terrain of Race: Debate over Whether to Chart Differences." *New York Times* 20 July 2001: A17.

Wallace, Michele. "The Hottentot Venus." *Village Voice* 21 May 1996: 31.

———. *Invisibility Blues: From Pop to Theory.* London: Verso, 1990.

Watson, Paul. "There's No Accounting for Taste." *Trash Aesthetics: Popular Culture and Its Audience.* Ed. Deborah Cartmell, I. Q. Hunter, Heiki Kaye, and Imelda Whelehan. London: Pluto, 1997. 66–83.

Weldon, Michael. *The Psychotronic Encyclopedia of Film.* New York: Ballantine, 1983.

White, Patricia. *Uninvited: Classical Hollywood Cinema and Lesbian Representability.* Bloomington: Indiana UP, 1999.

Wiegman, Robyn. *American Anatomies: Theorizing Race and Gender.* Durham, NC: Duke UP, 1995.

Williams, Linda, ed. *Viewing Positions: Ways of Seeing Film.* New Brunswick: Rutgers UP, 1994.

Williams, Patricia J. "The Contentiousness of Their Character." *Nation* 4 Jan. 1999: 10.

Williams, Raymond. "Argument: Text and Performance." *The Twentieth Century Performance Reader.* Ed. Michael Huxley and Noel Witts. London: Routledge, 1996. 369–83.

Wray, Matt, and Annalee Newitz, eds. *White Trash: Race and Class in America.* New York: Routledge, 1997.

About the Author

Gwendolyn Audrey Foster is an associate professor and a member and fellow of the graduate faculty in the Department of English, University of Nebraska-Lincoln, specializing in film studies, cultural studies, and postfeminist critical theory. Foster has published *Women Film Directors: An International Bio-Critical Dictionary* (Greenwood Press) about the history and critical reception of women filmmakers in the United States and abroad, and *Women Filmmakers of the African and Asian Diaspora: Decolonizing the Gaze, Locating Subjectivity* (Southern Illinois University Press). Her other books include *Captive Bodies: Postcolonial Subjectivity in Cinema* (State University of New York Press); *Identity and Memory: The Films of Chantal Akerman* and *Troping the Body: Gender, Etiquette, and Performance* (both from Southern Illinois University Press); and *Experimental Cinema: The Film Reader* (Routledge). Foster is also editor-in-chief of *Quarterly Review of Film and Video*.

INDEX

Stone, Sharon, 124
Stratemeyer, Edward, 133, 134
Stuart, Randy, 86
Studlar, Gaylyn, 140
Subjectivity: denial of, 63, 98; dynamics of,
    98; fantasy and, 99; female desire and,
    108; instability of, 68; white, 53, 108;
    working-class, 76
Subor, Michel, 111
Sullavan, Margaret, 118
Survivor (television), 124, 125
Swayze, Patrick, 9
Swerdlow, Joel, 151

TalkBack Live (television), 27, 28
Tarantino, Quentin, 64
Tarzan, the Ape Man (1932), 5, *12*, 13
Taubin, Amy, 111
Taylor, Kent, 85
Taylor, Libby, 36, 37
Television: minority representatin on, 94;
    nuclear family on, 123; reality,
    124–125; whiteface and, 4
Temptation Island (television), 124
Ten Commandments, The (1956), 61
Terminator, The (1984), 131
Terminator 2: Judgment Day (1991), 131
Terror, white consciousness and, 77
That 70's Show (television), 142
Thing, The (1982), 52
Thing with Two Heads, The (1972), 88,
    90–92
Tierney, Gene, 102
Tissot, Jacques-Joseph, 58
Toler, Sidney, 140
Tomb Raider (2001), 18
Trader Horn (1931), 8–9
Transgendering, 7
Transvestism, 7
Trevor, Claire, 124
Trinh T. Minh-ha, 138, 149
Tucker, Chris, 10
Tucker, Sophie, 36
Turner, Lana, 120, 124
Two of Us, The (1967), 84
2001: A Space Odyssey (1968), 130

Valderrama, Wilmer, 142
Van Cleef, Lee, 127
Vaudeville, 26, 33
Veblen, Thorstein, 108
Velez, Lupe, 142
Venter, Craig, 19
Vickers, Yvette, 73
Vincentelli, Elisabeth, 111
Voodoo, 130

Wade, Nicholas, 20
Wagner, Robert, 23
Walken, Christopher, 127
Walker, Texas Ranger (television), 142
War of the Colossal Beast (1958), 69, 71–72
War veterans, 71, 72, 75
Washington, Denzel, 9, 94
Watermelon Patch (1905), 65
Waters, Ethel, 126
Watson, Paul, 69
Weakest Link, The (television), 124–125,
    126
Webb, Clifton, 127
Weber, Lois, 99
Weissmuller, Johnny, 11, *12*
Weisz, Rachel, 7
Weld, Tuesday, 120
Weldon, Michael, 78
Welfare Reform Act (1966), 123
Wesson, Tina, 125
West, Mae, 34, *35*, 36–37, *38*, 39–41, 43
Wever, Sigourney, 130
What Ever Happened to Baby Jane? (1962),
    127
What's the Worst That Can Happen? (2001),
    10
White: "acting," 68; audience, 50; colonial-
    ism, 11; consciousness, 77; culture, 48,
    129; desire for servants, 131; fear of
    loss of domination, 17, 21; female
    decency, 33–34; female goodness,
    99–102, 105; heroes, 133; heteroper-
    formativity, 9; human race defined as,
    48, 49; identity, 26; as moral, 50, 122;
    as other, 11; passing as, 68, 89; patri-
    archy, 43; power, 32, 64, 66, 71, 86;

White *(continued)*
   privilege, 5, 7, 8, 25, 30, 37, 93, 98,
   103, 143, 150, 152; science, 86; subjectivity, 53; supremacy, 39, 48, 64, 66,
   146; trash, 143, 151
White, Patricia, 1, 5, 6, 21, 39, 43, 46
Whiteface, 3, 47–66; erasure of ethnicity
   and, 47; homogenization of performance, 53; identity claims of, 51;
   immigrants and, 52; lack of cultural
   scrutiny of, 4; lighting and, 4, 8; makeup in, 4; space ownership and, 51;
   white space as space of, 51
White Heat (1949), 127
Whiteness: acceptance of construct of, 4;
   allure of, 102–103; artificiality of, 4,
   20; association with death, 71; black
   film and, 67; brutality of, 85–86; citizenship and, 26, 30; coded as civility,
   54; critique of, 146; as cultural construct, 1, 2; darkness within, 82;
   dependence on blackness, 66; disavowal of hybridity and, 90; dualism of, 82,
   85; elimination of ethnicity and, 90;
   evils of, 147; false stabilization of, 18,
   25, 72, 73, 77; fear of diminishment
   of, 86; films working against, 67; as
   form of social control, 26; goodness
   and, 23, 48; heterosexuality and, 7;
   integrity of, 69; inventing, 25–46;
   invisibility of, 66; lack of ethnicity in,
   94; as legal construct, 30; maintenance
   of, 53, 54, 63, 86; motherhood and,

118–124; as negation, 5; as norm, 48,
62; othered, 5, 73, 90; performance of,
1–24, 32, 47, 51, 54, 61, 68, 73, 82,
88, 102, 131, 140; problematizing,
67–68, 72; respectability and, 41;
shifts in, 125; single motherhood as
threat to, 123; as social construct, 15,
25, 30, 103
White space, 3, 47–66; nature of, 50; post-
modern definition of, 50; as space of
whiteface, 51
White Zombie (1932), 128, 129
Widmark, Richard, 127
Will & Grace (television), 151
William, Warren, 105, 118
Williams, Grant, 86, *87*
Williams, Ife, 5
Williams, Patricia, 68, 78
Wilms, André, 145
Wilson, Dooley, 9
Winters, Roland, 140
Wood, Sam, 118
Woods, Tiger, 94
Wray, Fay, 8
Wray, Matthew, 32, 66, 77
Wycherly, Margaret, 127
Wymark, Patrick, 82

X Files, The (television), 10

Zucco, George, 129
Zukor, Adolph, 101
Zulu's Heart, The (1908), 65